AN
IN   EAR
BARTRAM'S
TREE

AN
IN EAR
BARTRAM'S
TREE

Selected Poems 1957-1967
by JONATHAN WILLIAMS

Introduction by Guy Davenport

"If I might bring you what I do—not so frequent to trouble you—and ask you if I told it clear, 't would be control to me. The sailor cannot see the North but knows the needle can."
—EMILY DICKINSON

THE UNIVERSITY OF NORTH CAROLINA PRESS
CHAPEL HILL, 1969

The number of my friends—current, quondam,
and worn—instrumental in publishing,
criticising, and airing many of these poems
is legion. They have my thanks and they know
who they are . . . Others in the Literary
Merchants' Sodality and numerous Urban
Wolf-Packs, as well as all but about 5000 of
the Body Politic, did nothing—and I expect
them to continue. Onword!

CONTEMPORARY POETRY SERIES

FOR: RONALD JOHNSON

let us call it Arden
& live in it!

IN LIEU OF A PREFACE:
The Poet's Emblems to be Writ Large
Across the Broad,
Vacant American Skies Every Dawn

Aesthetics is for the Artists like Ornithology is for the Birds.
—— BARNETT NEWMAN

Responsibility is to keep the ability to respond.
—— ROBERT DUNCAN

Great things are done when men and mountains meet;
this is not done by Jostling in the Street.
—— WILLIAM BLAKE

Now I am ice; now I am sorrel.
—— HENRY DAVID THOREAU

I am that he whose brains are scattered endlessly.
—— WILLIAM CARLOS WILLIAMS

Do not spoil your nature. But don't ask me what nature is
either. There are supposed to be above 200 definitions of it—
one is good enough for me.
—— EDWARD DAHLBERG

I do the very best I know how—the very best I can; and I mean
to keep doing so until the end. If the end brings me out all
right, what is said against me won't amount to anything. If the
end brings me out wrong, ten angels swearing I was right would
make no difference.
—— ABRAHAM LINCOLN

Stand up and use your ears like a man!
—— CHARLES IVES

The poet is the man who puts things together.
— BUCKMINSTER FULLER

A pine tree is not an oak tree.
— LOUIS SULLIVAN

Ja wohl, mein nomme is not Anton Bruckner.
— ERIK SATIE

I don't know
what the left is doing,
said the Right Hand,
but it looks fascinating.
— JAMES BROUGHTON

We may eventually come to realize that Chastity is no more
a virtue than Malnutrition.
— ALEX COMFORT

They ought to tear you down and put up a new building!
— GROUCHO MARX

90% of the worst human beings I know are poets. Most poets
these days are so square they have to walk around the block
just to turn over in bed.
— KENNETH REXROTH

The food of the Soul is Light and Space.
— HERMAN MELVILLE

The song is heat!
— CHARLES OLSON

Craft is perfected attention.
— ROBERT KELLY

To write a symphony means to me to construct a world with all
the tools of the available technique. The ever new and changing
content determines its own form.
— GUSTAV MAHLER

*The time will come when a single original carrot will be
pregnant with revolution.*
— PAUL CÉZANNE

*You can't derail a train by standing directly in front of it,
or, not quite. But, a tiny piece of steel, properly placed . . .*
— ROBERT CREELEY

Dig and sow!
— ABBOT LUAN

*Nature & Art in this together Suit:
What is Most Grand is always most Minute.*
— BLAKE

*The poet, no less than the scientist, works on the assumption
that inert and live things and relations hold enough interest
to keep him alive as part of nature.*
— LOUIS ZUKOFSKY

*All I ever did was make a little noise for some guys that
nobody was listening to.*
— EZRA POUND *(in conversation, Venice, 1966)*

*The world is full of strangers,
they are very strange;
and I shall never meet them—
it is easy to arrange.*
— FLORINE STETTHEIMER

Odi et amo!
— CATULLUS

*Whether it is fun to go to bed with a good book depends a great
deal on who's reading it.*
— KENNETH PATCHEN

DEGAS: *Voila, I've got this great idea for a poem!*
MALLARMÉ: *Alors, mon ami, poems are made out of words, not ideas.*

Just get the right syllable in the proper place.
— JONATHAN SWIFT

QUESTIONER: *If you had your life to live over, what would you do differently?*
W. C. FIELDS: *I'd live over a saloon.*

More light!
— GOETHE

What is the answer . . .? What was the question?
— GERTRUDE STEIN *(last words)*

If you don't know, why ask?
— JOHN CAGE

To live is to defend a form.
— ANTON WEBERN

Music is to make people happy.
— BUNK JOHNSON

Madame, may I ask of what else should Miss Sitwell's poems consist but 'words words words'—dead larks, tea cozies, antimacassars, and fragments of a stage elephant????
— OSBERT SITWELL

What to such as you anyhow such a poet as I? therefore leave my works
And go lull yourself with what you can understand, and with piano-tunes,
For I lull nobody, and you will never understand me.
— WALT WHITMAN

He speaks stones (so said Agrippa) and let his readers beware lest he break their heads.
— ROBERT BURTON

INTRODUCTION

JONATHAN WILLIAMS, poet. He is an entertaining array of other things, too, but they are for the historian of publishing to talk about, the connoisseur of fine books, the biographer, the raconteur, the chronicler, if any ever comes forward, of the poets who in our new intellectual ecology have risked their stomachs, nerves, and reputations to read in colleges, YMCA's, high schools, YWCA's, filling stations (yes, filling stations), universities, YMHA's, churches, and even department stores. There is a reason for this goliardry, to which we shall return. It was R. Buckminster Fuller, on his way from Carbondale to Ghana (and deep in Kentucky at the time) who remarked of Jonathan Williams that "he is our Johnny Appleseed—we need him more than we know." He publishes poets, introduces poets to poets, poets to readers, professors to poets, poets (perilous business) to professors, and he photographs poets. The color slide, descendant of the magic lantern, is still the most charming disseminator of culture, and Jonathan Williams is its master. He is the iconographer of poets in our time, and of the places and graves of poets gone on to Elysium. He is an ambassador for an enterprise that has neither center nor hierarchy but whose credentials are ancient and respected. He is also a traveller, hiker, botanist, antiquarian, epicure, and much else to engage our attention if we wish to look at the poet rather than the poetry. And so, quickly, before the poet gets in our line of sight, the poetry.

Its weightlessness is that of thistledown and like the thistle it bites. Its coherence is that of clockwork, at once obvious and admirable. Its beauty is that of the times: harsh, elegant, loud, sweet, abrupt all together. The poet in our time does what poets have always done, given a tongue to dumbness, celebrated wonderments, complained of the government, told tales, found sense where none was to be perceived, found nonsense where we thought there was sense; in short, made a world for the mind (and occasionally the body too) to inhabit. Beauty, poets have taught us, is the king's daughter and the milkmaid, the nightingale and the rose, the wind, a Greek urn, the autumn moon, the sea when it looks like wine. None of which appear often in the confusion of our world. Yet, perhaps all too rarely, poets keep to their traditional loyalties—

> dawn songs in the dews of young orange trees;
> and ranging orisons; and wordless longings
>
> sung in tranquillity's waters sliding in sun's
> light;
>
> and benisons sung in these trees. . .

That cello passage is Jonathan Williams meditating on Frederick Delius. The imagination of the poet converses with the imagination of the composer. The language for talking to Delius is Delius. And what if the poet wants to talk back to the TV set? It is there that he encounters of a morning rockets blasted toward a star his ancient craft has sung for two thousand years (and probably longer). He switches from cello to clarinet, piano, snare drum, and trombone:

> Woke up this mornin',
> Cape Canaveral can't get it up. . .
> Woke up this mornin',
> Cape Canaveral can't get it up. . .

> But sent a cable to Great Venus—
> told her, better watch her ass!

> *"Unravished bride of quietness,"*
> blasts off in my head. . .
> *"Unravished bride of quietness,"*
> blasts off in my head. . .

> Liable to be a whole lot more people
> than just John Keats dead!

Lonnie Johnson and Elmer Snowden, accomplished singers of the blues, were enlisted in this enterprise, for their tradition of eloquent dismay before a world independent of their will and opaque to their evaluation of life has been under refinement for three centuries, and their sly alignment of technology's troubles with a ribaldry both venerable and primitive is worthy of Brer Fox. The art of Méliès is there, too—the poet is remembering *The Rocket to the Moon* in which Verne's astronauts smack into the planet's outraged eye. And Keats' great ode. Poets are licensed idiots and can be counted on without fail to note the change when the silent moon—Sappho's wild-rose-fingered moon born from the violet sea, Vergil's friend of silence, Shakespeare's moist starre—becomes a junkyard.

The poet, like the horse, is a mythological creature. The accoutrements of both are the same now as in the days of Hsiang Yü, Mimnermos, and Caedmon. Their duties are the same, their *numen*, their intractable identity and presence. They are, they have always been. The horse is as archaic as he is modern, forever the "neighing quadruped, used in war, and draught and carriage" that Johnson said he was, independent of time and fashion: which is why the poet Christopher Fry called him the last mythological beast. Eternity seems to have made a separate contract with him, and extended the same gracious codicil to the poet, who also is neither archaic nor modern, or rather is most modern when he is most archaic. For the work of the poet is continuous while all other modes of discourse—mathematics, physics, politics—are wildly discontinuous, repeating stupidities because they forgot the past, stopping and starting because of barbarians, rebellions, and simple loss of vision. The poet works his melodies into the very grain of existence.

An eidetic Ezra Pound, we learn from the poem "Some Southpaw Pitching" in this volume, once appeared to the poet Charles Olson to say, *"Let the song lie in the thing!"* Our other recorded appearance of Ezra Pound as "a familiar compound ghost" was to Air Raid Warden Eliot during the Blitz when he could be discerned "in the waning dusk," along with Dante and Mallarmé, saying

> . . .our concern was speech, and speech impelled us
> To purify the dialect of the tribe
> And urge the mind to aftersight and foresight

Eliot of course is here re-imagining Dante's encounter with his teacher Brunetto Latini—the meeting to which the title of Jonathan Williams' first book alludes in its elate way, *The Empire Finals at Verona* (1959).

> Poi si rivolse, e parve di coloro
>   che corrono a Verona il drappo verde
>   per la campagna; e parve di costoro
> quelli che vince, non colui che perde.

The ghost also said to Mr. Eliot: ". . . next year's words await another voice." Another master to whom Jonathan Williams has listened with care wrote: "No ideas but in things." That was William Carlos Williams (no kin), who appears in this volume saying (in "Dangerous Calamus Emotions"):

> "him and that Jesuit, them with the variable feet—
> they changed it!"

Walt Whitman, he means, and Gerard Manley Hopkins. What they changed is what Jonathan Williams (with help and in good company) is still changing: poetry. "Next year's words await another voice." By paying careful attention to William Carlos Williams, who insisted that the poet's business is to let the world speak for itself, Jonathan Williams learned to make such poems as this:

> Mister Williams
> lets youn me move
> tother side the house
>
> the woman
> choppin woods
> mite nigh the awkerdist thing
> I seen

The title to this poem is a verbal gesture alerting us to cock our ears: *Uncle Iv Surveys His Domain from His Rocker of a Sunday Afternoon as Aunt Dory Starts to Chop Kindling.* The poem defines a culture. Edwin Markham was satisfied to let the man with the hoe remain as voiceless as the Barbizon painting in which he found him. That the world they have been so diligently describing might have a voice seems to be a late idea to American poets. James Joyce offered as the purpose of literature the simple but radically unassailable office of making the dumb to speak. And not in paraphrase. The poet locates himself between reality and the poem, and trains himself to be the medium through which reality flows into the poem.

> *I found the poems in the fields*
> *And only wrote them down*

That is John Clare as he speaks in Jonathan Williams' "What the Flowers in the Meadow Tell Me." And there is a response:

> John, *claritas* tells us the words are *not* idle,
> the syllables are able
> to turn plaintains into quatrains,
> tune *raceme* to *cyme, panicle* and *umbel* to
> form corollas in light clusters of tones. . .

> Sam Palmer hit it:
> "Milton, by one epithet
> draws an oak of the largest girth I ever saw,
> 'Pine and *monumental* oak':

> I have been trying to draw a large one in
> Lullingstone; but the poet's tree is huger than
> any in the park."

> Muse in a meadow, compose in
> a mind!

Any poem worth its salt is as transparently complex as

> air in a hornet's nest
> over the water makes a
> solid, six-sided music

wherein every quality is mirrored in another (and an *aria* and a *horn* are camouflaged into the richness); that the lines are typographically isometric, seven-syllabled, and inwardly ornamental (-net's nest, solid/sided, *s, m,* and *n* so placed as to make a bass line to the treble) is as native an instinct to the poet as the hornet's hexagonal architecture.

Native, to be certain, but only after much work. Man is the animal that chooses its instincts through emulation, and all his learning has roots and branches. Jonathan Williams' first masters would seem to be Charles Olson, whose *Maximus* poems he later published and whose master was

Ezra Pound. We cannot draw a direct line of descent from Pound to Olson, however, for there is an intervening generation. Louis Zukofsky and William Carlos Williams are at its center, its Mallarmé and its Whitman. Their admonitions to the young stressed objectivity, technique, honesty, clarity, realism. The European poem was not to be continued in America; it was not republican. Rhyme was feudal; recurring metrical patterns warped thought and natural speech. Images must come not from books but the world. The poet must therefore find a new shape for every poem, and liberty turned out to make far harder demands than the sonnet. Hence Olson's heroic struggle with balance of phrasing, William Carlos Williams' plain carpentry and boyish honesty, and Zukofsky's daredevil integrity and fierce control of rhythm and design—a passionate mathematics engraved on steel with a diamond. Never before had American poetry worked with such fine tools or insisted upon such craftsmanship. Professors of literature, ever conservative, cautious, and lazy, will discover all this in their own sweet time.

The young poets who went to school to these hard masters—Robert Creeley, Robert Duncan, Jonathan Williams, Robert Kelly, Ronald Johnson—have by now each evolved a style of his own. The spare asceticism of their training remains, however, as an armature within. Jonathan Williams learned how to write a poem as trim and economical as a tree. And like a tree his poems have roots, exist against a background, and convert light into energy. And take their shape not only from inner design but also from the weather and their circumjacence.

Which brings us to the fact that the honey bee has a lethal sting. Were it not for a long and distinguished history of poets who have balanced a love affair and a feud with the world—Archilochos, Catullus, Horace, Villon, Pope, E. E. Cummings—Jonathan Williams' double-threat handiness with a lyric would seem charmingly schizoid. *Odi et amo.* A settled hatred for one's species (Little Harp's excuse for his *terreur,* and his last words) is traditionally counterpoised in the satirist by a rich sensuality before all that's innocent.

The satire has been there from the first; wit and sense do not exist apart from each other in Jonathan Williams' mind. Pathos must appear in comic socks or not at all. Incongruity seems to be the stuff of existence, and outrage may be our surest response to the universe. There is a moral discourse of some consequence in the poet's reply to political rhetoric:

> Hush, L'il Guvnuh,
> don't you fret. . .

The genius of Jonathan Williams' satire is as old as tyranny. The slave learns to speak in riddles and sly enigmas; *The Blue-Tailed Fly,* homely folksong as it seemed, was in fact a song of emancipation. Look hard at the satires in this volume: their pungency and sass are not irresponsible, nor their wit flippant. In "Faubus Meets Mingus during the Latter's Dynasty" the particular politician and composer easily translate into the struggle between power and art anywhere. It is Jonathan Williams' surest instinct that poetry is not ideas or rhetoric. He locates meaning specifically. To the child's question,

> what fer
> thesehyar
> animules
> be,
> Granny?

the reply is:

> haint fer
> to name! why Adam's
> Off-Ox
> in thishyar
> Garden
> haint got
> no name
> neither
> yet
>
> but the Lord's
> liable to call
> thishyar
> tree
> Arber
> Vity
>
> hit's got
> thishyar
> sarpint
> in it

"And out of the ground the LORD GOD formed every beast of the field, and every foule of the aire, and brought them unto Adam, to see what he would call them: and whatsoever Adam called every living creature, that was the name thereof. . ." The child who inquired about the gingham and calico animals in the patchwork quilt will have heard these words in Sunday School and may never hear Milton's

> The grassie Clods now Calv'd, now half appeered
> The Tawnie Lion, pawing to get free
> His hinder parts, then springs as broke from Bonds,
> And Rampant shakes his Brinded main; the Ounce,
> The Libbard, and the Tyger, as the Moale

Rising, the crumbl'd Earth above them threw
In Hillocks; the swift Stag from under ground
Bore up his branching head

nor Jules Supervielle's

Sombres troupeaux des monts sauvages, étagés,
Faites attention, vous allez vous figer.
Ne pouvant vous laisser errer à votre guise
Je m'en vais vous donner d'éternelles assises.
Les chamois bondiront pour vous. . .

but has his vision all the same of the Garden, its Tree, and its Serpent.

As we read into this collection we become aware that whereas the satirist's predilections are as esoteric as the headlines in this morning's newspaper, the lyricist's predilections begin to display a wonderful strangeness. A pattern of artists emerges—Blake, Ives, Nielsen, Samuel Palmer, Bruckner—and (if we have our eyes open) a whole world. It is a world of English music, especially the Edwardian Impressionists and their German cousins Bruckner and Mahler, of artists oriented toward Blake and his circle but going off by centrifugal flight into wildest orbits, men like Fuseli, Calvert, and Mad Martin. The poet's admiration for Edith Sitwell will have had something to do with this exploration of English eccentricity, and the poet's Welsh temperament, and, most clearly, William Blake himself. The artist is aware of a heritage not only because, like the rest of us, he recognizes in it his origins and values, but because he is consciously adding to it. What Jonathan Williams found in England, Wales, and Scotland was not a second heritage (as it might seem to a casual glance) but the heritage in which he was raised from the beginning. When, for instance, he met the Scots poet Ian Hamilton Finlay, among whose work we can find (in the Glaswegian tongue):

hooch
a heilan coo
wis mair liker
it
    the hiker
s
hoo hoos
ferr feart
o ma
herr-do

he was, as perhaps only a citizen of Appalachia can know, solidly within his heritage. Finlay probably got his matter out of the air (the *heilan coo* can be found in his *Glasgow Beasts, an a Burd, Haw, an Inseks, an, Aw, a Fush*) without necessarily knowing that he was retelling a song that can be traced to Taliesin (the *Câd Goddeu*), is known in Spanish, Italian, Roumanian, Greek, and Serbian versions, and is sung in Jonathan Williams' neck of the woods as "She looked out o the winder as white as any milk."* Finlay has remarked of the Glaswegians that their dialect parodies itself, so that arch comic banter has become the preferred mode of discourse. The same observation describes Appalachia, the linguistic horizon that Jonathan Williams has never cared to stray very far from.

English eccentricity goes back to the Druids and beyond—the Sutton Hoo jewelry discovered in 1939 looks remarkably as if it were what Jonathan Williams calls Theosophical Celtic Art Nouveau. From Blake's Ancients (Samuel Palmer and Edward Calvert) stems a tradition. The Rossettis belonged to it; Browning paid it his respects; but for the most part it is a tangled and untraced path in and out of official literature and art. There's Charles Doughty whom entire departments of literature university after university have not read, a state of affairs roughly analogous to a department of physics sublimely ignorant of Proteus Steinmetz. There's Stanley Spencer, J. R. R. Tolkien, Edith Sitwell. And Bruckner and Bax and John Ireland. And Odilon Redon and James McGarrell. And more—we await the historian of these visionaries. Literature, as Harry Levin is wont to say, is its own historian, and Jonathan Williams' honor to his spiritual forebears may be the beginning of a resuscitation. Meanwhile, we must recognize that they constitute a tradition, and that he has taken up their torch, and carries it to and fro in the United States. His *Mahler*, responses movement by movement to the ten symphonies, will mark (once the dust has settled) the introduction of Blake's Young Ancients to our shores, a hundred and forty years late. If Walt Whitman had married the Widow Gilchrist as she proposed, we should not have had to wait so long, perhaps. And that speculation makes it clear that I have wandered far enough into an unwritten history.

Poetry is always inviolably itself, and it is always something more. Jonathan Williams offers us in every poem a lyric line of suave clarity and a highly involved verbal harmony. The poem itself finds and articulates a single image or action. This is an art like pole vaulting: the center of gravity is outside the trajectory. Build-up and follow-through are not the poem, though the poem depends upon them; the one is in the poet's control, the other in yours. We are not surprised to learn that the poet is an athlete.

And the poet is a wanderer. If his poetry defines and extricates a tradition from the past, his wandering (as Buckminster Fuller points out) defines the curious transformation of the shape of American culture. There is no American capital; there never has been. We have a network instead.

---

* Ian Hamilton Finlay's little book is based on the transformation theme. The protagonist shifts shape from one animal to another for various reasons. See Buchan's *Ancient Ballads and Songs*, I, p. 24, and Child's *English and Scottish Ballads*, I, p. 244.

A French poet may plausibly know all other French poets by living in Paris. The smallest of American towns contain major poets, and all other kinds of artists. In no other country does such a distribution of mind appear. Milledgeville, Ga., contained Flannery O'Connor (and at one time Oliver Hardy); Minerva, O., Ralph Hodgson. Jackson, Miss., contains Eudora Welty; Rollinsville, Col., Stan Brakhage. If you know where Carl Ruggles lives, Ray Bradbury, Michael McClure, or Edward Dorn, you may count yourself a learned man indeed. For a decade now Jonathan Williams has made it his business to go from point to point on this network: there has been nothing like it since the mediaeval scholars who for want of any other means of communication wandered from university to university. His long zig-zag trips can easily be explained by noticing that he is a publisher of books unwelcome to commercial publishers (who are closer to the grocery business than to that founded by Gutenberg); by invitations from universities to read, show slides, lecture on book design, architecture, and poetry; and by the fact that to know artists and poets one has to go to Pocatello, Id., and Pippa Passes, Ky. The true significance of all this gadding about is this: the poet with his preternatural, prophetic sense knows that this is the way he must live. Buckminster Fuller, who has also been on the road for the same decade, knew why Jonathan Williams is there too for the simple reason that they are each in his own way doing the same thing. Each has perceived that all other lines of communication are overloaded. Anything worth knowing passes from one man to one man. The book is still a viable way of communicating, provided one has taught oneself to find the book one needs to read. It isn't easy. All the electronic media are a flood of noise. And no medium can replace what may be an essential need in the poet: an audience. Homer recited his poems to people who cheered and even gave prizes; at least they passed around wine. Chaucer read his poems in warm firelit rooms. Every line of Shakespeare was written to move a paying audience. The next time you read a slack, obscure, convoluted poem, reflect that it was written in an age when printing has replaced recitation, and that the poet cannot tell his good poems from his bad except by fortuitous criticism. Jonathan Williams' books have been published in fine editions, many of them collectors' items from the moment of their printing, and all of them by this time scarce. It is therefore not hyperbole to say that thousands of people have heard them at colleges and auditoriums (and at that one filling station) for every five who know them on the printed page. Their clarity to the ear and the inner eye has been tested in the classical weather of poetry, listening faces. This collection, chosen by himself, is the first to be offered to that charming fiction, the reading public.

GUY DAVENPORT

Lexington, Kentucky

FROM: THE EMPIRE FINALS AT VERONA

(1959)

*Fielding Dawson made the handsome drawings and
collages for this first 'proper' book. It was dedicated
to Louis Zukofsky, "who has been alive consistently,
with love and respect." Other mentors included my
teachers at Black Mountain College: Charles Olson,
Robert Creeley, and Robert Duncan; Catullus; and
Edward Dahlberg. The latter warned me—or, tried to:
"You must be mindful of the species of nihilism that
obtains everywhere at present. A copy of the Daily
Graphic, as one young man asserted, is not a classic,
but a foe of sensibility, human consideration for
others, and a courteous heart." He also asked me: "Do
we have to go to books to be assassinated? How much
loam, ordinary dirt, foliage, moss, and even the dead
carcasses of birds that once were jubilant, is in a
book? Whole islands that are composed of the dead
are today the loam and ground of the living." What
I was doing, essentially, was trying to use the 'junk' of
the Eyes & Ears of the World—and lift it. I said in a
Note to the poems: "Here the idiomatic attack is a
mixture of opulence and delicacy; up-tempo and
elegiac. John Lewis' piano more than Thelonious' or
Bud's. On occasions, like Roy MacMillan at second
base—able to make all the plays with a proper grasp.
Poems like these are, after all, imaginative seizures
from the World at Large, caught on the fly."*

Credo:

I do
dig Everything Swinging (thinking

as I do:

ah, art
is fro-

zen Zen)

Goethe said: Architecture is frozen music.

O For a Muse of Fire!

Date: Tuesday, May 13, 1958—
    a date previously memorable in history for the birth of
    Joe Lewis (1914),
    the Empress Maria Theresa (1717),
    and the beheading of
    Johan Van Olden Barnveldt (1619)

Place: Wrigley Field, Chicago, Illinois

Time: 3:06 p.m.; warm and sunny; breeze steady, right to left

Attendance: 5,692 (paid)

Situation: top of the sixth; Cardinals trailing the Cubs, 3–1;
    one out; Gene Green on 2nd

Public Address: "Batting for Jones, #6, Stan Musial!"

The Muse muscles up; Stan the Man stands in . . . and
O, Hosanna, Hosanna, Ozanna's boy, Moe Drabowsky comes in

2 and 2
"a curve ball, outside corner, higher
than intended—
I figured he'd hit it in the ground"

("it felt fine!")

a line shot to left, down the line,
rolling deep for a double . . .

("it felt fine!")

Say, Stan, baby, how's it feel to hit 3000?

"Uh, it feels fine"

---

*Only six major-league players in baseball history had hit safely 3000 times
prior to this occasion. The density of the information surrounding the event
continues to surprise me, rather belies Tocqueville's assertion that Americans
cannot concentrate.*

The Oldest & the Coolest

(for Archie Moore, on TV, post-Bobo Olson)

at 1:19
of the 3rd round—
the winner
and still
Champion
of the World!

busy, very busy, coming in:
"I set him up with a couple jabs and
he was right *there*; then
I hit him with a double righthand, I caught him with a left
hook . . .

whip/whap,
that's it!"

gloves cut off, ready to cut out, pocket
comb going *flip* 30 seconds later . . .

"yes, man, a nice fighter; yes,
he shook me once; yes a left (note I was
moving by then, man);
yes, slow canvas, man; yes,
Rocky next . . . why'd I stare at him, man? why, man,

the eyes are
the mirrors of the soul, man"

Whether the Ancient One was entertaining us with Melville, Shakespeare, Cervantes, or himself, we do not know . . .

The Adhesive Autopsy of Walt Whitman

"Gentlemen, look on this wonder . . .
and wonders within there yet":

"pleurisy of the left side, consumption
of the right lung,

general miliary tuberculosis
and parenchymatous nephritis . . . a fatty

liver, a huge stone
filling the gall,

a cyst in the adrenal, tubercular abcesses
involving the bones,

and pachymeningitis"

"that he was a Kosmos is a piece of news we were
hardly prepared for . . ."

Verbatim quotations from the Philadelphia and Camden newspapers.

The Look-Out Tower at Mount Venus, Louisiana

yes yes o lord yes, the bestest, sweetest
pussy
      ever said good-morning to a slop-jar!

you know:
          'nappy' pussy,
like counting
prayer-beads:

. . . . ( ) . . . .

Heard/found-object, from Clement, man-servant to Weeks Hall, at the latter's plantation, The Shadows-on-the-Teche, New Iberia, Louisiana, 1957.

The Chameleon

at 14 I decided it was avant-garde to dig
women

but, man if I were just the least
bit queer, boy, you know, man, wow,

and then some; but, like
I'm not, but

when I write *Dearest* to you in a letter, then
that's different,

isn't it?

A Vulnerary

(for Robert Duncan)

one comes to language from afar, the ear
fears for its sound-barriers—

but one 'comes'; the language 'comes' for
The Beckoning Fair One

plant you now, dig you
later, the plaint stirs winter
earth . . .

air in a hornets' nest
over the water makes a
solid, six-sided music . . .

a few utterly quiet scenes, things
are very far away—'*form*
is emptiness'

comely, comely, love trembles

and the sweet-shrub

The Grounds

the Left Foot hit,
            deeply implanted,
                        at the edge of the Garden,
and Garlic sprang up!

Legend is legion, engendering green in the groundwork we work
to prepare a Spring in ourselves; to air the sound
in ourselves.

Belovèd Andrew Marvell, restore the furrow and the elms,
and melody!

Lusters, stir the row! Poe's
Valley-of-the-Many-Colored-Grass became
the Vale of Arnheim. Potomac's Valley shall become
a domain we create, an inchoate
scene where snows wane
and bulbs burn under the winter ground.

At the margins of thought, on the margins of the river, the winter
surrenders to the hosts of Great Venus.

By the fires of her campgrounds her hosts
sing her Vigil:

            tomorrow shall be love to the lover,
            and to the loveless too,
            tomorrow shall be love!

We are where there is
a green ground—

            and singing!

---

*A poem for the prophetic Edward Dahlberg, who wrote me he felt "caught
in the middle between the Marxists who I think have killed letters and the
Cartels who have destroyed everything, the earth, the furrow, the elms, human affections, the liver, and I think the pudendum too."*

The Sounds

A. Gordon Pym's Narrative;
Captain John Cleves Symmes'
"Theory of Concentric Spheres & Polar Voids"—

a day of white birds,
corpses of furry animals
with teeth
and claws

of coral red
                    . . . *Tekeli-li Tekeli-li*—unavoidable sounds,
sleet storms . . .
•
ice cracks down
among the hills
•
"the gazing eye falls through the world";
ubi amor, ibi oculus
•
I fix my eye, it runs along the ground, looking
for Masters of Language
•
"I have no designs on it, I can only say I
am involved"; "I write, as I can, stay in close, use
both hands,"
                    my Lady Ono Komachi,
                                        Edgar Allan Poe,
Tekeli-li Tekeli-li . . .
•
there is much
whiteness,
            and voids, crumbling

second to
second

FROM: AMEN/HUZZA/SELAH

(1960)

Being Southern-Fried Dada, High-Coups, Blues &
Genuine (Love-Lifted) Clichés— that is what the
back of the book advertised. The front featured a
blow-up of Mr. Blake's Visionary Spectre that came
looking like Ben Franklin by Al Capp. The dedication
was to Stefan Wolpe, and Louis Zukofsky contributed
what he called 'A Preface?'. The blurb indicated that
the poems were local to life during The Last Days of
Black Mountain College, that they were meant 'to
delight' and that other Poundian function 'to debunk
by lucidity.' Catullus, Li Po, Buson, and Marvell—four
masters of delectation—were being read during the
writing. "None of the lingo seems very esoteric,
except where it means to be. A certain quality of
invention is demanded, particularly if we are in the
backwoods with only bottle caps and plug-nickel
words flashing at us like mica. Offense is provided for
those who will take same."

Hymeneal to Leap-Year

Io! Io! you
Yo-Yo

Go!

Syllables in the Form of Leaves

1.

Fox plus *Razor* equals
the *Eye*—

get sharp,
or you're dead

2.

Der Lenz kommt über Nacht, sagt
Li-Po to

callow pussy
willows

3.

Das Leben kann allerdings angesehen werden als ein Traum, a
succubus mused,
                 sliding down my private
waterfall

4.

Ein Vogel singt im Baum—Ja . . .
Ja . . . a

bud said,
swelling

5.

Flogged with a *februum,*
young goats
dance out of

old goat skins

6.

Skin back the year,
turn over,
          you new leaf,
ewe!

Great Gray Green Greasy

1.

put the blocks
to winter?

raising avocados indoors
is, ouch,
hard enough

2.

goosed lizards, leaping . . .

put them peapickin claws
whar they belong,
alligator!

3.

after while, crocodile . . .

Three Tavern Songs in the Late Southern T'ang Manner

1. TRUNKENE IM FRÜHLING (MY VERSION)

    or—who else go into the shrubbery
    muttering
    or shine the silver flashlight
    at the female dormitory,
    longingly?

             questions, questions . . . always
             constrictions—

                    ah, to sit
                    in the catbird seat!

2. AGAIN THE NIGHT!

    so the moon, as she rose
    red,
       swung clean, from the hill,
    but her face through the window had '*Heart of Kentucky*' on it, an
    obfuscation (always a mystery), a
    sour mash,
             like this typewriter
    crashing across the swampgrass,
    as if brushing it
    aside . . .

             and trees, goddamn everywhere,
             and figures of speech!

3. THE DESPERADO

so,
a bottle of bourbon on the top shelf, why
not?

or,
who are you, you
yankee, to ask *anything*?

you've been seeing too many drive-in movies;
that is,
nobody does,
in fact,
here,
drink—

only icewater, or
syllabub, sometimes,

in the gloaming,
tra-la

The Bachelor

another day another
hotdog

a matter not so much
of impeccable underwear, a

certain seediness—yes,

sometimes a beard, between
women

something,
anything
to be engaged at
strokingly

a fairer feed-back, O
thou multitudinous
Orb!

Maniacs & Clown-Chasers, the Man Said

I want you boys to live in my town, I *mean*
Rose
        would take care of you!

Like a restaurant, you go back
to the back room, go
upstairs, yep . . .

                THERE IT IS ! ! !

                a pint on the table, piccolos
                playing,

                and four or five—
                just like they came into the world!

That's it,
boys

The gent who spieled this to me and Dan Rice one day in Ma Peak's Tav-
ern was an alcoholic who snuck over from the V.A. Hospital regularly for a
few quick ones.

The Midnite Show

Red-Wigglers, Night-Crawlers
& Other Worms
look out
into the crapulous moonlight:

figures of women cascading through the Sunday night;

no beer in sight.

I remember the *'Night-Blooming*
Cereus' by Dr. Thornton, Engraver, Blake's
patron, it
hangs in the hall outside the bedroom
swaying hungrily like these
giant white goddesses of the dark grotto . . .

there are touring cars
and men with large guns
singing through the woods

behind us.

The Bitch-Kitty

O Quondam Pre-and-Post-Bellum
Finger-Lickin Late Georgian Gentility!

this Lady thinks on Beauty, yes,
high cottons of Beauty up to
and including
the kazoo, bless
her Cottonpickin
Soul indeed
on its avoidance . . .

hast thou not never,
O Nouveau-Riche Peach-Queen, yet paused
to smile upon the blooming earth?

not 'just divine' but *green*

(*I find you highly offensive, suh*, she
said)

O green as goslinshit, and fertile
to the poorest Muse!

Free Admission Reptile Garden

the mind is, or might be,
                          a rattle, or
nest of,

          hung on the tail
of some snake
                    (parading dangerous, dull phlegm,
only . . .

so assumed, it whirs through a shimmer of an inspired
piss off a tin-plate,

and it struts dins blares
the wild farrago

and/or it leadeth into temptation, and
I shall not want
it,

    particularly

A Little Tumescence

this time, I mean it:
twice tonight!

> (*omne animal*, always
> The Hope

triste, triste
situation, such outrageous
limitation,
limp,

    simply

The rooster, post-coitum, is an exception— it laughs.

Finger Exercises

went down to the
boneyard
to buy a pair of hands, to quote
Robert Creeley

Olson wrote about Marsden Hartley's
hands, how they got,
refusing women's
flesh

and yes:
Hands, by
Sherwood Anderson,

hot to grope
blueberry, blacksuited
Ohio

arma virumque cano!—
plus the law's got a long
arm

we are too much in the hands of
those on whom we lay
no hands

The Anchorite

quotes Basil Bunting from "Chomei at Toyama":
if you can keep straight you will have no friends
but catgut and blossom in season . . .

the anchorite
opts to eye the
oak leaf, clutch
a red
to hold the mountains' blues
under the winter sun . . .

song accumulates heat—a humus. I have it,
like Issa:

> *Few people;*
> *a leaf falls here,*
> *falls there*

>   —outside, where
> the world's a storm
> in the oaks

> and the outcry of certain
> beautiful captures

•

he wrote 'brought to love,' brought to any
intimacy,
       writing letters
among red oak leaves . . .

to be left alone?—that's a laugh! that is, who's
without the images of
love,
     shining out of his head?

and they
who move the heart, daringly,
as the sun fires the oak
through the wanton afternoon
•
light airs of music . . .

we are left with
just the 'facts', the endless

articulation

Hojoki

no loot, no
lust to string a catgut
in a banjo

to hoot
or holler into
Nawth Jawja

too effete to
chant "Chattahoochee"
in trochaic feet

all's quiet at
Hut City

I have, in fact, stayed at length at a hermitage in Habersham County, Georgia, overlooking the rock upon which Mr. Sidney Lanier allegedly wrote his tedious, famous poem. This eyrie on Tray Mountain was larger than Chomei's 'ten-foot-square hut', but I imagine quieter.

Enthusiast

literature—the way we ripen ourselves
by conversation, said
Edward Dahlberg . . .

we flower in talk, we slake
our thirsts in a brandy of heated speech, song
sweats through the pores,
trickles a swarm
into the sounding keyboard,

pollen falls
across the blackened paper . . .

always idle—before and
after
the act:

making meat
of vowels
in cells
with sticky feet

A Spin

I cut the stuff,
a whole blue field: figwort
's what they call it

this particular day I put a car through it,
very fast,
out the gate, second gear, sharp right—

right out of ourselves also say,
a few miles only, but

quite out, and up:

Highest Point East of South Dakota, it said:
6684 feet,
oldest mountains on earth, etc.,
for what's in that

What good is a mountain without people? was all
he could ask

sure, it's what I mean—
if not, to hell with it!
I can, he said, regain composures,
and not only there . . .

The sun, suddenly hot on my hands,
holding the steering wheel;
the shadow of two ravens quickly across the car,
a dead raccoon by the road . . .

There are other things, I said, besides, say, air,
which, ok, you have to breathe, ok,
so also you gotta eat—like light or space,
or a mountain, very much,

which, if you'd climb the highest, works
well

FROM: ELEGIES AND CELEBRATIONS

(1962)

Another book including many very early poems. This one dedicated to my parents, "who first read me Baum, Lofting, Tolkien, and Grahame." There were rock photographs by Aaron Siskind. In the blurb I said: "Odi et amo, wrote Catullus. Nobody has said it any better. These poems, then, decry and exalt . . . I attend my demotic, unliterary ear, which has got big eyes for this American place. Until they build fall-out shelters for rattlesnakes and boll weevils, I'm not buying." In his Preface Robert Duncan wrote many memorable things, several of which remain very fixed in my head: "The accomplishd thing remains amazing: that this style permits busy effect, passionate utterance, cool and hot jive, right scattert insight, and nice discrimination to co-exist. Permits? demands. It is the demand that makes its path poetry . . . These poems outlive me as I read. They are not comfortable . . . The assertion by which the dilettante true to his delecto moves into the passion of beauty is the strength that moves us."

The Distances to the Friend

Thoreau,
        grabbing on, hard,
a red, raw
            muskrat . . .
thought to eat it,
                stifling all repulsion

so sat by the quagmire,
cranky, no cannibal, too
uninvolved
            to get to man
so simply

we, the
heirs, hear other rustlings:

the grass stirs like an
androgyne,
the man
in our hearts stands
his fear
on its head,
savagely—

            inversed, nervelessly,
we sweat past each other,
unrelieved:

bitter landscapes,
                unlovely

Dangerous Calamus Emotions

"Walt Whitman is in town—
I have just seen him, but
publicly of course."

> traffic jam! tram drivers,
> > streetcar conductors,
> > Sergeant Tom Sawyer, Peter
> > Doyle, all
>
> > the Camerados & Lovers

> DO NOT TALK TO DRIVER
> WHILE BUS IS IN MOTION, do not motion
> to driver, or
> bus will talk; walk, do not run
> to the nearest; and do not buss
> bus drivers!

deliver us, deliver ass
from puritan transit!

W.C.W.: "him and that Jesuit, them with the variable feet—
    they changed it!"

variable, viable,
veritable Walt

Whitman!

The initial quotation is from the sedulous Mr. Emerson to the prissy Mrs. Emerson, one of the New England gentry who did not approve of Whitman's athletic, amative, democratic tastes . . . Dr. Williams is referring to Whitman and Gerard Manley Hopkins—for him the founders of the modern poem.

The Big House

(for Sherwood Anderson)

plant
        candles about you,
dance nude through Wisconsin,

prance
        to the factory,
feeling the cloven hoof root
flowers
            about the business shoe . . .

see no one, ever more,
makes mess upon thy temple floors!

cast celebration
                like a seed!

To Charles Oscar

may there be stiff reeds
for your hands
among the asphodels,
Charles

and wind
to move them
over the bronze water
onto paper

and Lethe for us,
left
with your shattered
inkstone

_____

The painter, Charles Oscar, who did the drawings for my Four Stoppages
(1953), was murdered in New York City in 1961.

The Problem

I can stand anything
                          except the color of

        that butterfly

            flying
                  through those aspen trees

—which is *sensuality*
(albeit trees
have no faces in the Schwarzwald,
noted D. H. Lawrence)

a droning
off fields in Baden,
from gray violets pressed in a letter,

the grasses . . .
                (mingling closely the fingers of the hand)
clouds . . .

another man's wife, who has written:

"everything very soft . . . so calm . . ."

completely impossible

Those Troublesome Disguises

sat Will & Kate
                doing a Mr. & Mrs.
Eve & Adam . . .

Milton got murmured
                   like Bees
lost in the Hercules
Apartment's
              Eden-type Pavilion . . .

"Come on in, Nobodaddy here
but us
Chickens, Naked as
Jaybirds . . .

"Just Glimmed a Ghost, Man, the Most Gross
(like a Common Man would—a Lower Visible:

Scaly! Speckled! & Very
Awful!)

"We're Cooling it, Man,
Before the Fall . . ."

The source of this anecdote is to be found in Alexander Gilchrist's authoritative Life of William Blake.

The Tag Match

you know
           what I mean? I mean

why I call
Creeley 'Crippler
Carl',
      the Judo Chop
Specialist, cuts
content the best
two out of
three,

      falls: a multiple
          crash victim—
          staggers, fits &
          starts
          across a clean white page . . .

but then, friend, when
you're really in
the thing, then you do go, that's
for sure, not for
nothing, not for no one,
for your selva oscura, for instance,
obviously not

tis the ladies (The Late Ease)
selah, set
the feet
      one after another, a-
wondering whilst
wandering

god—even for a camel:

a mile!

Some Southpaw Pitching

(A Riff for Charles Olson via Charles Ives)

"let the song lie in the thing!" there's
music in anything! anything?

o there's poetry
in Mississippi; *exempli gratia*, the Iuka Drive-In:

I PASSED FOR WHITE plus
SNOW WHITE AND THE SEVEN SHADES

agreed?

Ives pitched for Hopkins Prep and beat
the Yale Freshmen and maybe pitched for Yale and beat
Dartmouth

once he stood in Dartmouth Common by the bon-fire
and heard the Glee-Club sing
"Where O Where Are the Pea-Green Freshmen?"

Ives, who knew how to take a lot off his knuckler,
took a lot off the tune, turning it
into the 'Allegro' of the *Symphony #2—*
and Dvořák can't beat it

so, let the song lie in the ear, if it
hears it

where o where are the pea-green freshmen
d'antan?

even Helen Trent has gone to hell
in a boat,

where we all float—

or don't

———————

The Shade of Ezra Pound once appeared to Charles Olson and uttered
the poem's vatic first line. No one has quite understood what he meant,
but it sounds like Heraclitus.

Ruggles' Visionary Spectre in Vermont

spoke its bit from
Blake:

> *Great things are done when Men & Mountains meet;*
> *This is not done by Jostling in the Street.*

see page 661, Centenary Edition, where Will
also celebrates

> an Ass,
> a Hog,
> a worm,
> a Chair,
> a Stool

—clearly the preferential

> if one be Artist in
> the reign of
>
> Crippled Harry & Slobbering Joe ! ! !

that new sound was 1949—Nature (the Wilde One)
imitates Art again . . .

the *Organum* of Ruggles and Carl Ruggles walks
out of the hills into
Carnegie's Hall

> (the urbane sit on their
> hands
> hoping for Benjamin
> Britten)

I think he walked all the way from Arlington, Vermont,
across invisible mountains
to take that unseen bow
with Leopold Stokowski

and how *nobody*
knew this

it is to sound
such unknown men
I write—

> albeit this act but
> jostles in the Modern Street,
>
> a rude distraction

Five Trail-Shelters From the Big Pigeon to the Little Tennessee

1. DAVENPORT GAP

the tulip poplar is not a
poplar it is a magnolia:
liriodendron tulipifera.

the young grove on the eastern slopes of
Mt. Cammerer reminds me
of the two huge trees
at Monticello, favorites
of Mr. Jefferson;

and of the Virginia lady
quoting Mr. Kennedy:

the recent gathering of
Nobel Prize Winners at the
White House—the most
brilliant assemblage
in that dining room
since Mr. Jefferson
dined there

alone . . .

a liriodendron
wind, a liriodendron
mind

2. COSBY KNOB

DeWitt Clinton (besides
looking like Lon
Chaney on tobacco-tax stamps)
comes to the eye
in *clintonia borealis*—

of which fair green lily
there are millions
on this mountain,

it is a mantle
for fire-cherry, yellow birch,
and silver bell

3. TRI-CORNER KNOB

here the shelter's
in a stand of
red spruce and balsam fir

for dinner: lamb's-quarters,
cress from the streams
on Mt. Guyot,
wood sorrel, and
cold argentine beef, chased with
tangerine kool-aid

4. FALSE GAP

no *Schwarzwald* stuff,
keine Waldeinsamkeit,

no magic grouse, no
Brothers Grimm—just
Canadian hemlock, mossed and lichened,
like unto maybe
Tertiary time . . .

too much for a haiku?
you hike it and see

5. SILERS BALD

just in front of the
round iron john
in the beech grove

the fresh bear droppings
give you

something
to think about

IN ENGLAND'S GREEN &

(1962)

*Subtitled 'A Garland and a Clyster', this volume was
superbly published by Dave Haselwood's Auerhahn
Press (San Francisco) and marks the first occasion I am
'all there' in my own voice and mature style.
Philip Van Aver did the remarkable drawings; the
collection was dedicated to Edward Dahlberg, my
continuing mentor, who'd reminded us all: "That
there are no Absolutes is of no importance; but he
who refuses to strive after them is a liar, a coward and
a caitiff." These are springtime poems, written during
five days of March in the Blue Ridge— hopefully a
tonic for evil humours, black bile, and urban demons.
The poems are also 'about' England, as it existed in the
imagination of a poet who had not yet been there in
person. John Wain noted: "Poets dream creatively of
Provence or Sligo, as boys in London live
imaginatively in the American west, jazz-lovers in
New Orleans circa 1905, and Sinologues in a
vanished Peking of blossoms and imagist poems."
Abbot Luan remarked: "Dig and sow." Gardyloo!*

Reflections from "Appalachia"

(In Honor of Delius' Centenary: 1962)

dawn songs in the dews of young orange trees;
and ranging orisons; and wordless longings

sung in tranquillity's waters sliding in sun's
light;

and benisons sung in these trees . . .

in these, yes, it is the 'ah-ness', yes, it is the course of adrenalin,
but, it is the lens opening of Frederick Delius' luminous blind eye:
f/stop open—
all things measureless lucidities,

my eyes
so in tune: atonement, at-one-ment is
atonement,

what is meant by not
being able to focus two eyes . . .

they lie on the horizon,
they lie on the great St. John's River's waters
in the monocular sunlight

three miles wide
lid to lid

Four excellent books on Delius (1862–1934) are Frederick Delius, *Sir
Thomas Beecham (Knopf, New York, 1960);* Delius as I Knew Him, *Eric
Fenby (G. Bell & Sons, London, 1936);* Frederick Delius— Memories of My
Brother, *Clare Delius (Ivor Nicolson & Watson, London, 1935); and the early
Delius by Philip Heseltine, now reprinted by Hogarth Press, London.*

Two Pastorals for Samuel Palmer at Shoreham, Kent:

1. "IF THE NIGHT COULD GET UP & WALK"

    I cannot put my hand into
    a cabbage to turn
    on the light, but

    the moon moves over
    the field of dark cabbage and an
    exchange fills
    all veins.

    The cabbage is also a globe
    of light, the two globes

    now two eyes in
    my saturated
    head!

2. "ONE MUST TRY BEHIND THE HILLS"

    Eight Great Dahlias stood
    beyond the Mountains

    they set fire to the Sun
    in a black wood
    beyond the Mountains,

    in the Valley of Vision

    the Fission of
    Flowers

    yields all Power
    in the Valley of Vision

    eight Suns,
    on eight Stems,
    aflame!

Readers are referred to Geoffrey Grigson's two books: Samuel Palmer's
Valley of Vision *(Phoenix House, London, 1960), and* Samuel Palmer: The
Visionary Years *(Routledge, London, 1947). My titles are from letters by
Palmer to George Richmond.*

❖❖

Beside the Fount above the Lark's nest in Golgonooza

Golgonooza?
Georgia?

You think Great Blake didn't know Enigma,
Alapaha, Sappville, Ty Ty, and Glory
were on Route 82, across south Georgia?

You're right, there's a lot Great Blake didn't know about—
larks' nests for one thing. Sing,
Rara (English) *Avis*

> ("me immense world of delight;
>   me unclosed by senses five"),

rave on!

Let's us talk about cardinals—*Richmondena cardinalis*. Let's, because in the midst of writing this poem, which is to be very
pedantic and mildly arcane and written very quickly to get rid
of worrying just for once whether it is prose or its blessed contrary, here is my old friend the cardinal pecking and pecking at
his rival's red image in the newly washed window. He sits in the
dry vines. I don't know the name of the damn vine, but it's there,
it's been there nineteen years since we dug a root from my great-
grandmother's farmhouse after her funeral and planted it.
Planted it *votively*. Great. I know that now but I didn't have to
know it then.

❖❖❖

O Linnaeus (always some taxonomist bugging us): "this
is the great alphabet: to affix to every object its proper
name."

Ok. *Richmondena cardinalis*, get your ass
out of mine nameless vine, nine feet above
my asarum canadense!
(Kinda dense, huh? Just wild ginger.) Prose or

poetry? Where are we? With emblems and birds,
and no fount—not in Golgonooza
at all.

Capital b-i-r-d-s: *Birds*, how do these airy spirits
stand it, O Despond?—they have never heard of
Odilon Redon
or George MacDonald or Denis Saurat, and think *Blake* sounds just
as good as *fount* in

Golgonooza.

The title, from Blake's "Milton: Book the Second" . . . There is a take on
birds from Blake's "The Marriage of Heaven and Hell." Much of the poem
derives (most deviously) from a reading of Saurat's Gods of the People *(John*
Westhouse, London, 1947), and Ruthven Todd's Tracks in the Snow *(Grey*
Walls, London, 1947)— two very excellent works.

Blues for Lonnie Johnson

> *"If you don't like my peaches,*
> *baby, don't you shake my tree."*
> — Orpheus

Woke up this mornin',
Cape Canaveral can't get it up . . .
Woke up this mornin',
Cape Canaveral can't get it up . . .

But sent a cable to Great Venus—
told her, better watch her ass!

"Unravished bride of quietness,"
blasts off in my head . . .
"Unravished bride of quietness,"
blasts off in my head . . .

Liable to be a whole lot more people
than just John Keats dead!

Got us a brand new play-toy,
and the Green Bay Packers too . . .
Got us a brand new play-toy,
and the Green Bay Packers too . . .

Same old incestuous, eschatological, lunatic football
Apollo's used to.

Some of Lonnie Johnson's best singing is on BLUES & BALLADS (Pres-
tige/Bluesville 1011), where he is accompanied by Elmer Snowden . . . The
poem suggests it would be nice to save the moon and other, as yet presum-
ably wholesome, places from John H. Glenn and Jesus H. Christ.

The Electronic Lyre, Strung with Poets' Sinews

(for Elizabeth Sewell)

> *"Orph's awfully gay,*
> *despite Eurydice."*
> — The Oracular Cave at Antissa:
> 'Music, Every Hour on the Hour'

Hey, Dead-Head,
Maenads got your tongue?

You go dead inside
and think you could

con me, the Shade
of Sigmund Freud?

Be polymorphous perverse,
Orpheus!

All orifices,
Orpheus!

"It's all good."

(signed)

God.

Ps/ *"Sappho died the other day . . .*
   all ass is gruss, so let's make hay!"

The poem may suggest an impious reading of three primary source books:
Miss Sewell's The Orphic Voice *(Yale, New Haven, 1961), Norman O.*
Brown's Life Against Death *(Modern Library, New York, 1959), and Jane*
Harrison's Prolegomena to the Study of Greek Religion *(Meridian Books,*
New York, 1955) . . . Shakespeare and John Cage are vaguely evoked . . .
The postscript, an epigram I covet violently, is by Mr. Keith Camp, John
Barton Wolgamot Fellow in Poetry, Ann Arbor, Michigan. Salute!

A Collect Night-Letter for Mr. Arthur Golding

... "EXILED
    AWHILE

    TO ISLE
    OF CAPRI,

    PERFERVID,
    IVIED OVID—

    TOO TOO AVID—
    EVIDENTLY

    HAD HAD IT
    UP CUPID ..."

    (U.P.I.:
    3 B.C.)

Ovid was exiled to Tomi, to be precise about it ... Golding's beautiful translation (1567) of the complete Metamorphoses *is back in print as "Shakespeare's Ovid" (Southern Illinois University Press, Carbondale, 1962).*

Cobwebbery

the best spiders for soup
are the ones under
stones—

ask the man who is one:
plain white american

(not blue gentian red indian yellow sun black carribean)

hard heart, cold
mind's found

a home
in the ground

"a rolling stone, *nolens volens,*
ladles no soup"

maw, rip them boards off
the side the house

and put the soup pot on

and plant us some petunias
in the carcass of the Chevrolet

and let's stay here
and rot in the fields

and sit still

———————

*The Lawrence quote is from his introduction to Edward Dahlberg's first
novel* Bottom Dogs *(City Lights, San Francisco, 1961). He spoke of the
American character . . . 'nolens volens': willy-nilly.*

A Mathom for J.R.R. Tolkien

on the streams of Westernesse outside the Shire
the Pipe-Weed grows with the Golden-Seal . . .

do not forget this in your zeal:
the emperies of elves *and* men are flowers!

shun Ranunculus at Raven Knob,
and Black Cohosh and Columbine
and Rue-Anemone—

the human minions/
the elven votaries!

beware the Hellebore
on Rabun Bald, or Barad-dûr, or Erebor!

A 'mathom', as defined in the Hobbit-lore of The Lord of the Rings *(3 volumes: George Allen & Unwin Ltd, London, 1954), is something for which there is no immediate use, but which one is unwilling to throw away . . . The plants invoked are all members of the family Ranuculaceae (Crowsfoot) to complement Raven Knob. The latter is in Rabun County, Georgia, as is Rabun Bald, third highest mountain in the state. Barad-dûr is the Dark Tower of Mordor; Erebor is the Lonely Mountain of Dale . . . I take the opportunity to re-affirm that Professor Tolkien's trilogy is the most magical work of the age. I began reading him at age 8—even that wasn't soon enough.*

The Flower-Hunter in the Fields

       (for Agnes Arber)

a flame azalea, mayapple, maple, thornapple
plantation

a white cloud in the eye
of a white horse

a field of bluets moving
below the black suit
of William Bartram

bluets, or "Quaker Ladies," or some say
"Innocence"

bluets and the blue of gentians and
Philadelphia blue laws!

high hills,

stone cold
sober

as October

Bartram's name to the Seminole was "Puc-Puggy," the Flower-Hunter.
He remains one of the very few great men to have visited the Florida
Lotophagoi since Cabeza de Vaca . . . I am most indebted to Mrs. Arber for
the two books of hers I know: Herbals *and* The Mind and the Eye (*both*
Cambridge).

The Familiars

(for Geoffrey Grigson)

in the Appalachians
we plant a campion,

a "Rattlesnake-Master."

Master Thomas Campion,
plant your garden in our face,
turn all our thoughts to eyes,

> Where we such pleasing change doth
> view
> In every living thing,
> As if the world were born anew
> To gratify the spring.

O Starry Campion, *silene
stellata,*

laudamus te, benedicimus te ! ! !

•

today is March twenty-first; the temperature sixty-one . . .

masses of rattlers as large as wash tubs,
as large as watermelons,
lying in the sun by their dens.

the Indian said:
deer and ginseng and snake are allies
avenging each other;

but it is another, Spring Rain, god of rattlesnakes, puts
their signature
on the plantains by the ledge.

laudamus,
Crotalus horridus
horridus!

lead us
into the crevice into
the central den!

•

our insufflator, the warm sun,
warns us of the excrescences of language—

ecdysis, exuviation, desquamation—
it's the words that need to be shed.

so we coil on the stones with our blue eyes
calling for Mnemosyne to install
a new endothermal
control,

for the myth was: the shed skin was
immortal

(afflatus filling the skin
in the wind at night).

"the skinne that ye snake casts in ye spring tyme, being sod in wine,
is a remedie for ye paine in the eares"

—Dioscorides

paeans in our ears!
Greek, Cherokee & United States of American Paeans,

that a caduceus of Viper's Bugloss
may cleanse our ears to hear—

even to the Language of the Birds!

for the Scripture is written:
"Plants at One End, Birds at the Other."
•

house-leek & garlic,
hyssop & mouse;

hawk & hepatica,
hyacinth, finch!

crawl, all
exits

from
hibernaculum!

This 'bookish' poem is derived from a variety of reading: James Mooney's
Myths of the Cherokee *(Bureau of American Ethnology, Washington, 1900),*
and Laurence M. Klauber's incredible Rattlesnakes *(2 volumes: University of*
California Press, Berkeley and Los Angeles, 1956) are the principal sources
. . . From Thomas Campion I have made several paraphrases and quoted,
almost verbatim, a stanza from Number XII of the Second Book of Airs *. . .*
The 'Gloria' I have in mind is that of Francis Poulenc . . . The quote from
Dioscorides is from The Greek Herbal *(Hafner, New York, 1959) . . . "Plants*
at One End, Birds at the Other"— from Saurat's Gods of the People. *He*
heard this in Hyde Park, London . . . "The Familiars," being dedicated to Mr.
Grigson, offers small thanks indeed for his extraordinary The Englishman's
Flora *(Phoenix House, London, 1955) and for his wide-ranging work as a*
whole . . . Lest I give the impression that these ten little poems are manu-
factured strictly from other literature, let me say that their spirit and ecology
derive from a summer's hike of 1457 miles along the Appalachian Trail—
Georgia to New York at the Hudson River at Bear Mountain, 1961. Since
walking is one thing and writing another, men's minds are better nourish-
ment for poems than raisins are.

FROM: LULLABIES TWISTERS GIBBERS DRAGS

(1963)

*Poems á la manière de M. Louis Moreau Gottschalk,
Late of the City of New Orleans, written in
Stonegrave, Yorkshire on the afternoon of June 17th—
a serene place to produce such rude sounds but the
poems had their ears to the violence of the American
ground. They grew from two causes: (1) examining
the* Oxford Dictionary of Nursery Rhymes, *edited by
Iona and Peter Opie (London, 1951), on the train from
London to York; (2) my chagrin, as an American and a
poet, at being away from the United States when it
was time to stand up and be counted, lest one be
taken for not having lived at all or participated as
citizen or artist in the process of decency. The words,
here, are wielded like scalpels to rid minds of debris
and dead wood. I would like to think they are in a
viable tradition that includes Edward Lear, Christian
Morgenstern, Kenneth Patchen, and Stevie Smith—
if we had their songs in our nurseries, things might not
be so crazy. These songs need no apology except
William Blake's useful assertion: "Poetry Fetter'd
Fetters the Human Race." LTGD was dedicated to
James Farmer; the covers were executed by R.B. Kitaj.*

Lullaby for George Wallace
Up to the Ass of a Very Tall Indian
On the Banks of the Black Warrior River
In Tuscaloosa County

Hush, L'l Guvnuh,
don't you fret . . .

got you some wet dinnuh,
if you'll just stand aside:

weevils
riding a crimson tide—

smothered in suthun-fried
fratricide . . .

From Colonel Bert Brecht's Alabama Song Bag

lalla, lalla, alabama . . .
sing your song, old yellowhammer:

rock-a-bye, you baby buzzards . . .
basta, basta, alabastards!

―――――――――

I am thinking of the song in the Brecht-Weill opera, Mahagonny . . . *the Yellowhammer is the State Bird . . . there is the town of Alabaster south of Birmingham I drove through after I wrote the poem— one guess what the locals are called . . .*

Heart-Song Dear to the American People

don't let the sun set on your head! I said
to the golden rod

it stood
in the pine wood

out back
it was black

as a heart

Everybody Twist!

LAWLESS WALLACE ÜBER ALLES

all ass, alas,
no arse-
nic, no
lace,
as well as no
solace

no Ace Carter, no Bull
Connor

LAWLESS WALLACE ÜBER ALLES

White Anglo-Saxon Protestant Invocation; or,
Don't Let a Wet W.A.S.P. Get His Shit Hot

From Commies & Sheenies
and Bull-Dickied Darkies—

Good Lord, Deliver Us!

An Air-Express Collect, Fifty-Pound Watermelon
For Senator James O. Eastland

smile, Mr. Jim,
I want to see those false teeth
smile

 clear to the far side of Tampa Bay,

boy

I don't want to see nuthin
but elbows and assholes,

jowls, sow belly, and one dead
panatella

I want to see it *all*,
in tall cotton!

Riddling Fish in a Racist's Barrel in Creep County, Georgia

what do they call a colored paleo-climatologist down south?
— nigger

what has four legs and weighs 500 pounds?
— two 250-pound pigeons fed on Tennessee, Walking Horseshit

what *did* the Governor of North Carolina say to the Governor of
South Carolina?
— it's a mighty long time between finks

what do you call a seven-foot Negro carrying a bull-whip in
Maddox Country?
— SIR!

what has two seats and is made out of petrified wood?
— a John Birch birch john

what has one eye and comes in a white box?
— Sammy Davis, Jr.

what good is a white southerner?
— that's neither a riddle nor funny

Be My Bloody Valentine

necks are red, noses are blue,
Jim Crow's dead—how bout you?

Dealer's Choice and the Dealer Shuffles

(for William Burroughs)

I saw the Chattahoochee River get a haircut.
I saw Fidel Castro flow softly towards Apalachicola, Florida.

I saw a bank of red clay integrate with Jesuits.
I saw Bob Jones Bible University used to make baked flamingos.

I saw the Governor of Mississippi join the NAACP.
I saw a black gum tree refuse to leaf and go to jail.

I saw the DAR singing *"We Shall Overcome!"*
I saw Werner von Braun knitting gray (and brown) socks
      for the National Guard.

I saw the Motto of Alabama: "IT'S TOO WET TO PLOUGH!"
I saw God tell Adam: "WE DARE DEFEND OUR RIGHTS!"

I saw the City of Albany fried in deep fat.
I saw eight catfish star on Gomorrah TV.

I saw "THE INVASION OF THE BODY-SNATCHERS" at the
      Tyger Drive-In.
I saw William Blake grow like a virus in the sun.

I saw the South suckin hind titty.
I saw the North suckin hind titty.

I saw a man who saw these too
And said though strange they were all true.

Postface:

'There was a crow sat on a clod—
And now I've finished my sermon, thank God.'

FROM: MAHLER

(1964)

*In response to Duncan's admonition "Responsibility
is to keep/the ability to respond," I sat down with
earphones at the typewriter, listened to the forty
movements of Gustav Mahler's ten symphonies, and
wrote forty 'spontaneous' poems during May and
June. In Bruno Walter's words: "We must think of
everything that touches our hearts with gentlest
beauty and tenderest charm." R.B. Kitaj used the
poems as partial departure-points for a suite of
silk-screen prints, and the whole folio was published
in 1967 by Marlborough Fine Art Ltd (London and New
York) in an edition of 30 copies. The work was,
again, dedicated to my great friend, Stefan Wolpe,
whose music also honors Mahler's spirit.*

Symphony No. 3, in D Minor

> *"Thousands lavishing, thousands starving;*
> *intrigues, wars, flatteries, envyings,*
> *hypocrisies, lying vanities, hollow amusements,*
> *exhaustion, dissipation, death— and giddiness*
> *and laughter, from the first scene to the last."*
> — Samuel Palmer, 1858

I. PAN AWAKES: SUMMER MARCHES IN

Pan's
spring rain
"drives his victims
out to the animals
with whom they become
as one"—

pain and paeans,
hung in the mouth,

to be sung

II. WHAT THE FLOWERS IN THE MEADOW TELL ME

June 6, 1857, Thoreau in his *Journal*:

A year is made up of a certain series
and number of sensations and thoughts
which have their language in nature . . .

Now I am ice, now
I am sorrel.

Or, Clare, 1840, Epping Forest:

I found the poems in the fields
And only wrote them down

and,

The book I love is everywhere
And not in idle words

John, *claritas* tells us the words are *not* idle,
the syllables are able
to turn plantains in quatrains,
tune *raceme* to *cyme, panicle* and *umbel* to
form corollas in light clusters of tones . . .

Sam Palmer hit it:
"Milton, by one epithet
draws an oak of the largest girth I ever saw,
'Pine and *monumental* oak':

I have just been trying to draw a large one in
Lullingstone; but the poet's tree is huger than
any in the park."

Muse in a meadow, compose in
a mind!

III. WHAT THE ANIMALS IN THE FOREST TELL ME

Harris's Sparrow—

103 species seen
by the Georgia Ornithological Society
in Rabun Gap,

including Harris's Sparrow, with its
black crown, face, and bib encircling
a pink bill

It was, I think, the third sighting
in Georgia, and I should have been there
instead of reading Clare, listening to
catbirds and worrying about
turdus migratorius that flew

directly into the Volkswagen and
bounced into a ditch

Friend Robin, I cannot figure it, if I'd
been going 40 you might be
whistling in some grass.

10 tepid people got 10 stale letters
one day earlier,
I cannot be happy
about that.

IV. WHAT THE NIGHT TELLS ME

the dark drones on
in the southern wheat fields
and the hop flowers
open before the sun's
beckoning

the end
is ripeness, the wind
rises,
and the dawn says
yes

YES! it says
"yes"

V. WHAT THE MORNING BELLS TELL ME

Sounds, and sweet aires
that giue delight
and hurt not—

that, let
Shakespeare's
delectation
bear us

VI. WHAT LOVE TELLS ME

Anton Bruckner counts the 877th leaf
on a linden tree in the countryside near Wien
and prays:

Dear God, Sweet Jesus,
Save Us, Save Us . . .

the Light in the Grass,
the Wind on the Hill

are in my head,
the world cannot be heard

Leaves obliterate
my heart,

we touch each other
far apart . . .

Let us count
into
the Darkness

Symphony No. 4, in G Major

". . . inter urinas et faeces nascimur."
— St. Augustine

I. SERENE—WARY, NOT HURRIED

"Happinesses have wings and wheels;
miseries are leaden legged;
and their whole employment is to clip
the wings and take off the wheels
of our chariots.
We determine, therefore, to be happy
and do all that we can, tho' not
all that we would,"

said William Blake in Felpham, Sussex

And so there are
mysterious chariots chanting
charivaris and planting
haricots verts
in the air
over Thomas Hariot's Cheviot
potato patch

Everything should be
as simple as
it is,
but *not*
simpler,
agreed Professor
Einstein, a stone's throw
away in Chariot

Eight

II. IN A COMFORTABLE MOTION

"like a fiend in a cloud,"
Death calls the tune,
plays out of tune and arrives
in a cloud

heard only by the catbird,
who sits in Death's June sunshine
and sings the tune again

and again

and simply continues singing:

black eye/blue sky!
black eye/blue sky!

III. RESTFUL

"I live in a hole here,
but God has a beautiful mansion for me elsewhere."

O grow
a Mountain in Fountain
Court

Sundown over
London

Kate Blake
in black

IV. VERY COMFORTABLY

St. Peter looks on in Heaven,
6 O'clock, Sunday, the 12th of August 1827:

"Lest you should not have heard
of the Death of Mr. Blake
I have written this to inform you . . .

— Just before he died His Countenance became fair—
His eyes Brighten'd and He burst out in Singing
of the things he Saw in Heaven. In truth He Died
like a Saint as a Person who was standing by Him
Observed . . ."

No music on earth
is there
that might ever compare
with ours

Symphony No. 5, in C Sharp Minor

"How blessed, how blessed a tailor to be!
Oh that I had been born a commercial traveller
and engaged as baritone at the Opera! Oh that
I might give my Symphony its first performance
fifty years after my death!"
— Mahler, 1904

I. FUNERAL MARCH

Mahler, from his studio on the 11th floor of the
Hotel Majestic, New York City, hears the cortege of a
fireman moving up Central Park West:

one roll of the drum

one road where the wind storms, where
Cherubim sing birds' songs
with human faces and hold the world
in human hands and
drift on the gold road
where black wheels smash
all

one roll of the drum

II. STORMILY AGITATED

to be a block of flowers
in a wood

to be mindlessly in flower
past understanding

to be shone on
endlessly

to be *there*, there
and blessed

III. SCHERZO

one two three
one two three

little birds waltz to and fro
in the piano

at Maiernigg on the
Wörthersee

and up the tree:
cacophony

one two three

IV. ADAGIETTO

one feels
one clematis petal
fell

its circle
is all

glimmer on this pale
river

V. RONDO-FINALE

Schoenberg: "I should
even have liked to observe
how Mahler
knotted his tie,

and should have found that
more interesting and instructive
than learning how
one of our musical bigwigs composes
on a quote sacred subject
unquote

. . . An apostle
who does not glow
preaches heresy."

his tie was knotted
with éclat
on
the dead run!

RANDOM POEMS

Paean to Dvořák, Deemer & McClure

besides Beethoven and Brahms, Dvořák "studied
with the birds, flowers, trees, God, and
himself"

VHOOR ZHOCK!
VHOOR ZHOCK!
VHOOR ZHOCK!

I celebrate this Slavic creature
who so sang and loved America at a time
Henry James, Gent.
went around in a closed railroad car in Georgia lamenting
nobody cared, nobody cared, how dreary
the land was and
always would be . . .

1893, June: Spillville, Iowa:
the *F major Quartet,* "The American" (Opus 96),
composed in three days (!) in a village
composed of Czech immigrants and many
birds on the Turkey River

"a damned bird (red, only with black wings)" sang its way
into the *Scherzo*
and stayed there

(Spillville is between
Eldorado and Jerico
west of
US 52)

On the Continent the Quartet is called
"The Nigger Quartet"—

Ach, Meinen Damen und Herren, it was a
red bird not a black bird,
and your version of America is, as usual, absurd . . .

however, other ears were hearing the American land,
particularly, Mr. Charles Ives' . . .

he, as Lou Harrison says, 'decomposed' the demotic and found
music in the ground

but Dvořák took to the aire, his drone is the hive of melody
of a Bohemian's yearning, his discerning
of the American Grain Eden—
mellifluous and glorious, sad, sweet, strong—sung so
in the *Cello Concerto*
"Praise is the practice of art!"

WOOD/BIRD/GOD/WORD

HEARD WORLD!

•

my god I'd like to go to bed with everybody,
even with the chickens and with the moon and get up
like a sun!

let's all go to Oregon and eat
yard eggs, drink home-churned whole
buttermilk in stone crocks, bake
bread of whole-wheat flour—

and may orchards and rivers
ease us!

•

O Grass of Parnassus,
where have we been
(the bottle gentian
and I) all
your life?

"now I am ice, now
I am sorrel"—

Thoreau, clear as spring water, cog-wheel nature
fitted into the infinite
under his foot . . .

wool plus lichen plus human urine make
black tweed

so we take the Golden Road, the Road
to the Palace of Wisdom, we take the Walk
to the Paradise Garden

intent upon sorrel
like Angelico and Botticelli and
fertilized
by the smaller bees and flies . . .

Delius tells us, Blake tells us, the lake, the
catbird, the oak gall, the aspen, the plantain, the weed,
seed, jugs, clouds, fires,
thrones, thorns, mires, snakes
tell us:
We are the Ruination
& the Light!

it is simple-minded to say so,
it is single-minded to say so—
we ask to be close to those
who are lost here, they are our kinsmen:
lichen
alga
and *granite* . . .

work for the night is coming,
work for the night is coming,
work for the night is coming,
when man's work is done . . .

— Charles Ives worked that corny presbyterian hymn tune
into nearly every piece he wrote

you rust out or
you burn out

and if this be the last night,
let it be! see
how few
will grieve us:

alga?
lichen?
granite?

I have asked the wood thrush to bless us:

philos!
philos!
philos!

SYMBIOSIS WE PRAY!

SYMBIOSIS WE PRAY!

SYMBIOSIS WE PRAY!

Emblems for the Little Dells, and Nooks, and Corners of Paradise

> *"You have only to work up imagination to the state*
> *of vision and the thing is done."*
> — Blake, to Palmer

out of the stills of Habersham: occasionally
potable calvados;

out of the hills of Habersham: sham
trochees, Ol' Marse Sidney's poses, Poe's
memories of the Lost Lenore, ah, Last of the Cherokee Queens,
        elas . . .

alas,
no one has *yet* seen the Soqui River in Habersham County, Georgia
(not far from modern Lake Lanier) on a winter afternoon between
        the hills—

no one except its despisers, versifiers, fishers, hunters, dumpers
of inner tubes, runners of sugar liquor, and errant crackers,
who are
familiar Christian white folks with
red necks and blue
noses,

brown mule and
black hearts . . .

it is hard to see the Soqui River in the late red sun
of a December afternoon (I reckon not even
Henry James saw it!)—
it is too hard to atune to, or atone for;

it is a stone's throw across that dark water to
Secure, Literary Yesteryear: Palmer
speaking of "that 'stinking hole Shoreham' which indeed is now
highly scented with the buds of spring"

. . . everywhere and forever more everything's stinking, but thanks
for thinking of us, Sam,
standing there staring into the sun

with the apple trees sizzling and the Valley yelling FIRE,
for we are not troubled by problems of aerial perspective in
the Valley of Vision—

> Zion is in the Sun
> of England's
> Eden
> on the Darenth,
> Kent

and we can turn it into the moon of Bunyan's Beulah Land *and*
hear the voice of the Bard:

"the green mountains that glimmer in a summer's gloaming
from the dusky yet bloomy east;

the moon opening her golden eye, or walking in brightness
among innumerable islands of light,
not only thrill the optic nerve but shed
a mild,
a grateful,
an unearthly lustre
into the inmost spirits,
 and seem the interchanging twilight

of that peaceful country

where there is no sorrow
and no night"

roll the apple away from the tomb, put
an apple in the mouth of Stinking Lazarus;

put it in the sky,
make a moon of it!

we are willing to raise anything!

the nightingale is singing
on Hampstead Heath
141 years after the death
of Keats

tradition is in us
like the sun!

"sin is
separation"

―――――――――――――――――――――――――――

Beaucoup Buttercups

and   c o w   c o w   c o w
        o o   o o   o o
        w   w   w

    parsley parsley parsley

the way a
whole field looks
back at you

in Berkshire in
June

―――――――――――――――――――――――――――

The Inevitable Form of an Early Flying Machine

```
TATLIN
 ATLIN
  TLIN
   LIN
    IN
     N
     NI
     NIL
     NILT
     NILTA
     NILTAT
```

mantis
mandibles
in
sect-
ions

Tatlin
N's in
sections

in
Len-
in's
Plan
For
Monumen-
tal
Propagan-
da

(but can
it get
off the ground?)

A 75th Birthday Maze

```
B I T E
        D A M E
        S I T W E L L ' S
          T         L         A
        H O T                 C
            C                 E
        C   T
        O   O
        B   B
    F R E E
      A     R
      C
    F O R
      L
      A L L
```

Slab
(for Carl Ruggles)

ONE
TONE
ON
ONE
TONE
ONE
STONE
ON
ONE
STONE
ON
ON
ON
ON

Gardyloo! (A Salutation for Christopher Murray Grieve
On the Occasion of His 75th Birthday, August 11, 1967)

May Glen Fiddich trickle down the burns
and white roses replace heather!

May Burns, Dunbar, MacDiarmid
trickle in the minds
and climate replace weather!

May your conturbation
rouse the artless Nation!

"May your Bottom
never be used
to stretch a Banjo!"

— the latter toast
Chris Grieve gave me in Langholm,
presumably a gist
from the Gaelic-Scots, the original, alas,
now lost . . .

I salute his zest!

A FRENCH 75! (*Salut Milhaudious*)

Devout to art, never played out

Animé, like an aspen

Ragtime Polyphone of the Rhône and Roaring Fork

Illuminé, like Cézanne's mountain

Ubiquitous, in place, and always poised

Somnolent, like the machines sorting the paternal almonds in Aix

shaloM

amI

de Satie et ClaudeL

invigorator of the 'gloire' of mytH

éminence non-grise de la musique française, voilA

we salute yoU

Cher Maître et GranD

Written on the occasion of a Dinner given by the Board of Trustees of 'Music Associates of Aspen' in Honor of Darius Milhaud & in Celebration of His Seventy-Fifth Year, August 6, 1967.

Blue Ball Blues

(for Paul Goodman)

O, Mr. Chemist, please let me buy
350 pounds of premium Kentucky KY,

cause it's a dry season
for the reason

Anglo-Saxon sex glands
are awry . . .

Arise, arise and come
to Perineum

(*'the more you come
the more you can'*)

Let not your Sword sleep in your Hand
and we shall smear Petroleum
on England's Groin
& Pleasant Gland!

FROM: JAMMIN' THE GREEK SCENE

(1959)

This collection got as far as page-proofs but somehow got lost in the shuffle and never, in fact, was published. The 'facts' came out of Robert Graves, Ovid, and Jane Harrison; the idiom from Clifford Brown, Bud Powell, Blakey and Miles. The results suggest the time Aeschylus put megaphones in the hands of his thespian-type Errinys— six came on, screaming like fifty. People gave birth, etc., on the spot. I am also reminded that Hercules kept snakes around to lick his ears— it let him hear all the sounds, like all. Charles Olson's Note included these remarks: "What Brother Jonathan does in hyar is to keep up the velocity at the same time that the things are let be. Ganymedes, or Echo, or that one Io, get back, by vulgarism, their patent vector powers . . . Barbarism, neologism, vulgarism, these London better have her old ear out for. The soul sd Duns Scotus is on a rubber-band runs out the mouth and if you wake a body too quick . . . I'm sure we got askance from utter shyness. They made us shy, the whole thing fronted so. We winced. Now we's wincin' back. I mean, we's shy. Bro Jonathan, he shy. He's got these things where . . . We's bristletails and earwigs, most even at the feast." The covers were by Fielding Dawson.

The Case of the Castrated Space Cadet

1. MAN THE MAKER/

> via Uranus, Mother Earth
> knew what had hit her, he
> was right *there*, not (by way of her anus)
> the north wind, or blue river,
>
> a diet
> of beans, a stray
> grasshopper

2. THE TITAN FRAT/

> this young cat Cronos carries and edge,
> grabs Dad by the nuts,
> and cuts him

3. THE OLD CROW/

> Father Time still
> makes it, comes in cool during the
> Yule,
> snips the mistletoe
>
> sickle! sickle!
>
> the
> red
> drops

4. MEANWHILE, BACK AT THE RANCH/

> Miss Venus
> rides the edge of her sugardaddy
> sea, and foam
> enlivens the tides
>
> with eryngo and doves
> and hi-fi flute playing
> off Malibu
>
> they wash

"Always the Deathless Mu-Sick"

1.

Play, Orfeo, play!
put us way out of it

Birds, Beasts (who don't dig vibes the least) dig
Old Daddy-O

"Get tall, O Oaks—
the climb's on me!

2.

Orf's *awfully* gay,
despite Eurydice . . .

The Four Aces From Thrace wail
immortal lullabies at *Birdland* but

the square chicks stay
chill

who'll cut down that creep
in Slice City

3.

A-cephalous, off-key, Orpheus
floats out to sea, he

bleeds indefinitely

into the Egyptian Scene, seen
amidst Fire Island
Pharoahs & Lebesarians—

a multicolored, prognosticating
Wurlitzer

spin on, Orfeo, spin on . . .

The Priapupation of Queen Pasiphaë

say, lay
        off the doll biz, Daedalus,
construct me
                a stately mansion, dad, a conveyance
for my
        quote most monstrous lust unquote!

got just the rig, doll, try this
                                cow on—
for size . . .

o squeeze it, squeeze it, cool queen, it's ok, it's called
plywood—
            elastic and the latest!

ho! all's reet in Crete, daddio . . . so,
roll me over, into
the clover—
            thar whar that stud what's hung spiels
trash to them simple chicks,
                            you dig?

man, mused Minos, so she's
a bitch on wheels . . .

moral:

white bulls, sacred to Poseidon,
don't fool
that easy, that's
for sure—

which is sort of
the first cock & bull story

for sure

Hearts of Stone

the story that asks the question:

can this chick,
from a Little Mining Town in the West,
find happiness, as
the wife of

Very Noble, Matinee Idol

of a million other
women???
•
so enter Echo, on a nympho kick . . .

she tracks
Cousin Narcissus
into leafy tryst—"Sorry
I just don't dig chicks—
drop dead, Lady!"

ah, her bones, they say, were turned
to stones . . .

and shake, rattle,
roll and reverberate in fens,
glens, and generally
miscrable scenes
•
Silver Screen Upon the Wall,
Who's the Fairest Teaser of Them All?

hopeless, chivalrous Narcissus, the Inscrutable, turns
into a blue movie
                    (*The Ennui's On Me*)
star for stag
parties

sort of 'introspective' vehicles,
viz:

    "O Peerless Piece, why dost thou me thy lover thus delude," he
lisps, refusing even Hades' lips

                              for the Annual Laurel-Leaf Chewing-
                              Gum Box-Office Award

•

O unwept, et cetera—*and* unlaid . . .

Echo, ditto—grotto, *grotto* . . .

Ovid, Meet a Metamorphodite

Hermaphroditus, a delight, a
dreamboat on Lake Salmacis,

a dazzling dud
what wist not whut luv wuz

alas, a lout, the lass aloud allowed,
                              so far beside herself

that scarcely could she stay

so Sister Salmacis hides her in
a bushy queach
to glim the scene at Muscle-Beach
as Hermes, Junior, doffs
his dongarees

no fenny sedge, nor barren reek, no reed
nor rush, just

          SPLASH!

— and passion's double-clutched!

strive, writhe, wrest and struggle, unsnugglin' stranger, grins she
snake-like,
applyin' the boa bit . . .

Hermaphroditus?/Hismaphroditus?
butch?/bitch?
which twain has the gonē?

o, one'll get you two: a toy of double-shape—

the cream of
genes!

The Honey Lamb

the boysick (by gadzooks thunderstruck)
Rex Zeus, sex
expert, erects
a couple temples
                    and cruises the Trojan Coast . . .

eagle-eyed, spies,
swoops,
swishes into town

ponders, whether tis nobler
to bullshit, brown
or go down
on
      that catamite cat, Kid Ganymedes,
                              mead-mover,

erstwhile eagle-scout
bed-mate

That Old Original Phrygian Ball-Buster

Attis is
at it is
he?

— to quote Cybele, a Really Big Earth-Lady (she
too go off nut, she make much lamentations-like:

1) to make a totem of pine
   out that sweetheart of mine
   he cut off the
   old pine tree . . .

2) he's a sure nuf gone tomato, he's
   a busted valentine . . .

3) Attis-Kit/Attis-Kat—
   a green & yaller double-backed beastie
   in the form of a monkey
   on somebody's back . . .

come on friend,
gimme some skin!

moans the Magna Mater,
croon the Castrate Choir . . .

tambourines
and redder violets
in a bloody ditch—

ain't it a bitch!

Stag or Drag (Come As You Are)

testing, testing
               1 . . . 2 . . . 3 . . . 4 . . .
or, STOP ME BEFORE I THRILL MORE,
scrawled some maniac in Chicago,

like chicken
ain't nuthin but a bird, allowed
Actaeon, lounging
on a rock, getting his rocks
off

. . . faggots for god's sake (50! Dykes 50!), swimmin'
sequestered-like

you've had it, son, the Unhuntress Enchantress
Artemis mused, addressing
a meal-ticket—another good man

gone to the dogs

The Switch Blade (or, John's Other Wife)

men share perceptions (and
their best friends' wives, in lieu of

a perverse tangling of arseholes)

— so, if you don't dig that sound get down together
on the wrestling mat *mit* your
Blutbrüderschaft,

Mr. Caesar,
Mr. Seizure,
Mr. Man

(every man's woman and every
woman's man, said Suetonius)

yes, but:

Will Andrew Jones Join
the Androgynes?

play it as cool as you can, a pragmatic man said—

there is no end

to desire

Idyll

a soft heart and a hard
cod

song is down,
in the mouth,

heating

FROM: SANK-AUNT-SANK SHOWS

(1966)

*These minuscule poems were my response to a
call from Ian Hamilton Finlay to help him edit an
anthology of 350 one-word poems by 350 almost-
wordless poets as an issue of his magazine* Poor. Old.
Tired. Horse. *Being a mountaineer I have a
garrulous landscape nature that feeds on Brucknerian
lengths. But also, being a mountaineer, I have an
exactly contrary nature that yearns to be as laconic
as Webern or a pebble. Here, the titles work as
hinges to spring what follows loose. An ear is on the
prowl, prying into the substance of words, finding
things there while one eye watches and the other
wanders about a bit bemused. The dedication was
to Francis Poulenc— small homage for his beautiful
simplicities. He reminds us that the common is not
common at all. You must man your dictionaries
accordingly. Written September 1–8, the George
Inn, Hubberholme, Upper Wharfedale, West Riding
of Yorkshire.*

Curiosities of Ale & Beer From the Bickerdyke Chronicle

The Uneuphonious White-Ale of Cornwall:
laboragol

Quoting Pope, "The Clamorous Crowd Is Hushed With Mugs of:
mum"

In Vogue with the Roystering Blades of Former Times:
huff-cap

The Lucious Fluid Producing the Bloated Habit of Body of the
West-Country Connoisseur, Bones Phillips:
grout

An Ale Consumed With Gusto in Cymru:
cwrwf

The Beer of Barley, Cambridgeshire, That "Won't Let the People
Go":
Pharaoh

Drunk in the Country on Mothering Sunday:
bragot

A somewhat Remote Ancestor of Ruddle:
dogsnose

The Wassail of November First, Sacred to the Angel That Presides
Over Fruits & Seeds, 'La Mas Ubal':
Lambswool

The Very Writing of This Word Summons Visions of a Shining
River, of Shady Backwaters, of Summer Days, of Two-Handled
Tankards, of Deep, Cool Draughts:
shandy-gaff

Composed of Equal Proportions of "Old & Bitter":
mother-in-law

Roman Wormwood, Gentian Root, Calamus Aromaticus, Snake
Root, Horse Radish, Dried Orange Peel, Juniper Berries, Kernels of
Seville Oranges, All Placed in Beer, Plus a Pound of Galingale for
Taste, Become the Sublime:
purl

Of the Greatest Benefit in Incipient Consumption in 1744:
stitch

The Reputation for Being Most Excellent Tipple:
tewahdiddle

The Squeeze of the Crabs Growing in the Wild in the Woods
(Appropriate to Nations Who Have Made But Slight Advances on
the Path of Civilization):
cyder

Wilder Foods in Britain

for the really hip: *hop*

for the celestially stewed: *cloudberry*

for the panic-stricken: *capers*

for the dionysiac: *earthball*

for the faraway: *caraway*

◈◈◈◈◈◈◈◈

Adumbrations From Sheet 90 of the One-Inch Ordnance Survey Map

The School of Hard-Knox at:
Wham-Bottom

The W.C.T.U. Holiday Camp at:
Booze-Moor

The Alphabet-Soup Kitchen at:
Jinglepot

The Old Soldiers' Home at:
Studfold

The Field Named Haw-Daw at:
Giggleswick

The Great Pennine Way at:
Gaudy-Backsides

The Forthcoming Assignation at:
Hole-Ho

Hoare-House Common at:
Horsehouse

The Old Oaken Bucket in the Well of Loneliness at:
Hag-Dike

The Abandoned Porcelain Works at:
Crackpot

News From Other Small Worlds

A Louse of a German P.O.W.:

stalag-
mite

Down at the Formicary, Time Flies:

inst-
ant

The Favorite Drink of Scots Poets:

fly-
te

Be He Butterfly, Or:

be-
he-
moth?

The Future Goes Gadarene:

pig-
eon

❖❖❖❖❖❖❖❖

A Range of Ranges

Ancestral: *Grampian*
Fruity: *Appalachian*
Detumescent: *Cumbrian*
Callow: *Tyrolean*
Bloody-Minded: *Transylvanian*

Five Far-Fetched Literary Rambles

Noah (Webster) Counts the Animalcules Two-by-Two:
ab cd EF gh IJ KL mn OP qr st uv WX yz

Who, According to Coleridge, is the "Fair, Soft-Flowing Daughter
of Fright"?
Urine

What is the First Really Miltonic Adjective?
adamandeve

An Aspect of a Well-Hung Wallpaper in a Pre-Regency Gentile
Drawing-Room:
pre-
puce

Who said, Great Things Are Done When Sprouts & Mountains
Meet?
Cole-
ridge

❖❖❖❖❖❖❖❖❖❖

Petite (Wet) Suite

Sweet or Meat: *Tay*
Tiny: *Thames*
Grant Us: *Mersey*
Why Not?: *Wye?*
And So: *Forth*

FROM: 50! EPIPHYTES,-TAPHS,-TOMES,
-GRAMS,-THETS! 50!
(1967)

*A collection of bits and pieces, nicely printed by
Poet & Printer, London. Why are poems
'epiphytic'? Because they are, perpetually, making
it up out of the air. Dum spiro, spero, to quote the
motto of South Carolina, not a very hopeful place
at all. In an introductory note called The
Logodaedalist's Apologia, I noted that three or four
laureled spirits had been invoked and plundered:
Archilochos, Martial, Blake, and, from our own time,
J.V. Cunningham, whose epigrammatical power
often leaves me gasping, with aching teeth, etc. The
best epigram lately belongs to Igor Stravinsky
("Wagner is the Puccini of music."), but the wits
have been exercised here vigorously, and lapidary
care is the order of the day. This is not Laodicean
writing. As Robert Burton suggests: "If you like
not, get you to another Inn." The dedication was to
Kenneth Rexroth, whose epigram "Fact" is a fact
one can't improve on.*

William Blake

Defoe's & Bunyan's Company;
Bones & Fields for Calvary

Jocelyn Brooke

now no one sees
the dew on the hobble-gobbles*
in the beech lane to Bishopsbourne

----

*Kentish nickname for 'Lords and Ladies' (Arum maculatum)

Bob Brown

the Gastronaut took only
a bag of rosehips, the seeds

of a sunflower,

and two cheeses,
from Trinacria

Anton Bruckner

may the next sarcophagus engraver
at St. Florian's do better
than *'Professor Anton Brukner,
Docktor der Philosophie . . .'*

Gaius Valerius Catullus

I love and I hate
and that's all she wrote!

Frederick Delius

your Yorkshire
aires

of darkling
thrush

in dark ling*
brush!

_____

heather in the local dialect

Sir Edward Elgar

went wyde in this world wondres to here—
hill tune and wind song with Maluerne's* ear

_____

this spelling of Wm Langland's mediaeval demesne is according to the Rev.
Skeats

Rainer Maria Gerhardt

'an end, un-
expected

all of a sudden,
even

for himself'

Charles Ives

Where O
Where
are
the Pea-Green
Freshmen?

New Haven,
West Redding, and
Heaven!

All aboard!

Amen!

Leoš Janáček

I wanted to sink my eye
into the blue of the sky

Bunk Johnson

he died
like the moon

fading out white
before day

Mina Loy

'each sin, severally
sinned, or to be,
sinned
since the Fall'—

the pen was in
the glands of Bartholin

Gustav Mahler

the sun shone on
on one alone . . .

'*bless* relaxes'

Carl Nielsen

as if all the world
sang one fine tune!

Charlie Parker

turn on the Bird, the Bird
turns me on, even
the Early Bird
turns worms

Francis Poulenc

ô salades!
ô mes délices!

ô Sally!
ô Alice!

salut!
ô zut
alors!

Maurice Ravel

if Couperin could
write your monument,
he would

Erik Satie

sat at tea

Jean Sibelius

the drone of overtones in
a rye field by
a river

Jack Spicer

there was his poem
about the ugly gardener's son,
Crotchety Priapus,

weary in the weeds without the hots
for anyone

let's hope Death
has a big one
for Jack

Walt Whitman

good bie Walter dear*

---

*WW's mother was almost illiterate

William Carlos Williams: March 4, 1963

I like it
that you died

the month
spring comes

Three Herpetological Epigrams

1. TWO WAYS TO SEDUCE A MEDUSA:

   asp backwards; or, stoned

2. ON THE GENERATION OF VIPERS:

   'hestiasteris is a Persian plant,
   so named from its promotion of goodfellowship,
   because it makes the company gay;

   it is also called *protomedia* from its
   use to gain the highest position at Court'
   — Pliny: *The Natural History*

   'I found that their interests were very limited.'
   — W. S. Burroughs: *Junkie*

3. HOW ASKLEPIOS REMEDIED PANDORA'S BOX:

   gorgon orgone

Five Sit-Ins Agin Out'n Out S its

1. SCARLET O'HARA DIGS HIZTRY

couth
Sooth

(befo de Wa)

no
Ocacay
Olacay!

onay itshay?
Ofay
Lady

2. UNCLE TOM, THE PSALMIST SAYS:

some of you
Negroes

gwinna git us
niggers

killed

3. THE INTERSTATE POMEGRANATE

(for Igal Roodenko & Bayard Rustin)

Kora
in Hell;

C.O.R.E.
in Chapel
Hill

the Lady takes a back seat
for six months;

my friends refused a back seat,
got thirty days

4. FAUBUS MEETS MINGUS DURING THE LATTER'S DYNASTY

the late
etiolate

Orvile
smiles:

'Skin,
friend?

Arkan-
sasophile?'

'No, Melville's
Ofay Snowman, man!'

sang ten T'ang
tenors

(arcane
saxophobes)

5. THE AGONIZING & INCOMPLETE EVOLUTION OF SOUTH CAROLINA
ENTOMOLOGY:

chigger . . . . chigra . . . . Chegro

Bucky Fuller's Favorite Geodesic Recipe:

Chicken
Tetrahedron

Chef Henri Ragout's Old Reliable 'Poultry' (Chick) Stuffing:

bonehead, plus
pussyfoot

Perfect Heaven!

Virginia Gentlemen
prefer (KY) bourbon

Arsy-Turvy (or, Three-Inch Will Please a Lady)

Dearest Fame:
Please come!

There is nothing
here at all.

An Objectivist's Anthology:

1. Lou-
2. is

3. Zu-
4. kof-
5. sky

My Own Up-to-date Epitaph (Variation on Mr. Blake)

My title as a Poet thus is prov'd:
Not Prais'd by Creeley nor by Olson lov'd.

FROM: THE LUCIDITIES

(1967)

'Sixteen in Visionary Company,' written largely in
London in March, 1966, and in April during a walking
trip in Wales— a continuing exploration of the
luminous qualities in certain British artists— their
combinations of precise, hot, innocent observations
that produce at-one-ments in all our eyes. Omissions
like Richard Payne Knight, William Beckford, John
Brown, E.R. Eddison, Francis Oliver Finch, Francis
Danby, Charles Doughty, Richard Wilson, John
Crome, Turner, Constable, Stubbs, Fuseli, Francis
Kilvert, Gilbert White, Richard Jefferies, George
Herbert, Traherne, Clare, Smart, et al., will be
rectified in poems to come. John Furnival made the
line drawings. The dedication was to Guy
Davenport: "For what there is/ is much/ to very few."

The Fourteen-Year-Old Samuel Palmer's Watercolour Notations
For the Sketch, "A Lane at Thanet":

                grey sky
                mottled with blue &
                warmish light

this thatch
very bright

                      elder
                      berry very bright

              this
              little
              gate

            very bright

                  br. light

Palmer's sketchbook of 1819 has recently been acquired by the British Museum from the great-grandson of his younger brother, William. It has glimmerings of the visionary Blakean style evidenced in the famous sketchbook of 1824, and of the paintings in the "Valley of Vision," on the Darenth, Kent, 1824–34.

A Speculation on First Visiting the Tomb of the Centenarian
Sake Deen Mahomed, Shampooing Surgeon to George IVth and
William IVth, In the Churchyard of the Parish Church
Of St. Nicholas, Brighton, Sussex:

old

fat

and

hot

S.D. Mahomed (1749–1851) first introduced Turkish Baths into England.
In the Regency Society of Brighton and Hove's publication "About
Brighton" it says ". . . the patient was first steamed in intense heat till
he perspired freely and then placed inside a kind of tent for massage.
In this he was vigorously pummelled by an invisible person from the
outside, whose arms alone appeared through the tent."

A Vista of Galactic Catastrophe in the Manner of John 'Mad' Martin:

oi veh, o vampire
camp, o
Castle Drekula
in damp Transylvania ! ! !

the HORROR when
Himself flies in . . .

"Ja, It's Been
a Hard Night's Flight"

— and then:

the new cook
cooks
kosher ! ! !

See Catalogue:

#281: "Waiting for Death":
Thomas Bewick's Last Work
(Also His Largest: 11¾ in. by 9 in.),
Left Unfinished . . .

had for its object
to effect
a humane improvement
in the condition of
the Horse

the block,
very much cracked,
is now
in the possession of Mr. Thomas Gow . . .

Mr. Bewick, pronounced BUICK,
rests in the Churchyard at Ovingham,
pronounced
AH-VIN-JUM,
a part of the Tyne Valley
now occupied by Horsey
People who have hardly ever heard

of him

Bibliographical information is from the Catalogue of the Bewick Collection (Pease Bequest) in the Public Library, Newcastle-upon-Tyne, Northumberland, 1908. This 110-page work, with ten excellent plates, is still available at the original price: one shilling sixpence . . . Other information is from extensive walking, in the Basil Bunting Country.

The Triumph of Craft: A Vignette From the Hebrides
For a Home Arts & Industries Exhibition
As Arranged by Mary Frazer-Tytler Watts
Under the Elms at Compton, Surrey:

lad asks Bessie
the old lady
in the factory

well then, what do you do
with all that steel wool
you steal?

well then,
I'm knittin'
a kettle

Mary Watts, the young second wife of G.F. Watts, painter and Honorary President of the Anti-Tight-Lacing Society (Gertie Tipple, Secretary), in her designs for the Watts Memorial Chapel at Compton, near Guilford, Surrey, created one of the unique fantasies in all of architecture: Celtic plus Art Nouveau plus Obsessive Theosophical . . . Watts, himself, needs revision on the basis of such paintings as "The Sower of Systems," where he comes out minor-league Gustave Moreau. And, after all, to quote the authoritative words of Violet A. Wlock, B.A., Deputy Curator of the Castle Museum, York, 1939–47, in her "A Chat on the Valentine": ". . . crinolines are creeping their way to fashion, there is even a whisper of tight lacing . . ."

A Yell For the Greatest Terrible Writer in the World:

AMANDA! AMANDA!
SIS-BOOM-BAH!

MCKITTRICK! MCKITTRICK!
RAH-RAH-RAH!

ROS! ROS!
THE REST IS DROSS!

Jack Loudan's biography, O Rare Amanda! *(Chatto, London, 1954),*
is the proper introduction to the magisterial alliterations of Amanda
McKittrick Ros (1860–1939). There is nothing else like this tea-cozy
prose from Larne Harbor, County Antrim, Ulster. Read Irene Iddesleigh,
Delina Delaney, *and* Poems of Puncture. *Here is a quite ordinary passage*
from Helen Huddleston: *"Helen Huddleston's cleanly vessels were never*
smeared with the abominable phlegm of the profligate . . . her tiny feet
always pattered on the pavements of the pure." My discovery of Amanda I
owe to Arthur Uphill, of London, a rare and honored friend.

The Wreck on the A-222 in Ravensbourne Valley

"There are more things to love
than we would dare to hope for."
—RICHARD OF SAINT VICTOR

where the car hit him, fireweed sprang with
blazons of fennel

and umbels
of dill fell
through the spokes of a wheel

on Whitsun holiday to the sun, Denton
Welch spun a web in his crushed cycle,

sat in the seat, spine curled up like a spider—

and spied: "saw
the very drops of sweat glittering frostily
between the shoulder blades"

of a lad

. . . on and on he spied and bled from the blades of his cycle,
small as a spider,
hiding in the fireweed, getting
wet from the skins of many human suns aground
at the Kentish river near
Tunbridge Wells,

where the dill
lulls,

and all boys
spoil . . .

The dire chronicle of Denton Welch's (1917–1948) accident and illness is told in A Voice Through a Cloud, *originally published by John Lehmann in Great Britain, and recently republished in America by the University of Texas Press.*

Dirge for Seer-Scrivener, Prince-Plangent of Gormenghast

"And the days move on
and the names of the months change
and the four seasons bury one another
and the field-mice draw upon their granaries"

— this is the kind of vision
Mervyn Peake shares with William Blake:

seeing
not with
but *thru*
the eye!

you get it, very very steady
in the *Titus* trilogy—

one extraordinary instance being
that passage in Book One, pp 116–7,
where Steerpike spies the dead tree
high on the cyclopean walls
of Gormenghast Castle;

and in Book Two, Chapter Fifty-One, Section V:

". . . A loosened stone falls from a high tower.
A fly drops lifeless from a broken pane.
A sparrow twitters in a cave of ivy . . ."

I can do nothing but quote
this fantastic man, like Kenneth Patchen,
creator of one Dark Kingdom,
unstrung by a darker one . . .

I lament all ravens and the owls in hell
who stay his hand
and dis-connect this sun

---

*Mervyn Peake (1911—died November 17, 1968 at Burcot, Oxfordshire) was
perhaps the last master of gothic delineation and the grotesque, though his
prose comes from Melville and Dickens and not Mrs. Radcliffe. Because of
his disabling psychic illnesses we had no successors to the Gormenghast
Trilogy or to such illustrations as those to the "Ancient Mariner" or to
Alice in Wonderland. Like Delius, Poe, Lovecraft, Coleridge, his time was
no place for him.*

Thomas Johnes, Master of Hafod Ychdryd (The Summer Palace
By the Winding River), Cardiganshire/Eden

it must look today very much as Johnes first saw it,
seventeen-whatever it was . . .

some son of a bitch has, recently, made a killing off the lead rights
and cut the last of Johnes' trees

between October 1795 and April 1801
he planted two million sixty-five thousand trees,
nearly half of them being larch

for, outside the Domain of Hafod, Wales was like this,
to quote a much later account (1854) by George Borrow:

"much mire in the street;
immense swine lay in the mire . . .
women in Welsh hats stood in the mire, along with men
without any hats"

hee hee
hoo hoo
said the locals

that is Borrow at the Bridge of the Holy Ford,
on the way to Strata Florida, Vale of Flowers,
where he kissed the Yew-Tree, sacred to Davidd Ab Gwilym,
one of the first poets of the world

the locals
are still
cackling

but, back, the first Hafod burned, 1807
(a housekeeper's warming pan);
the famous library went sky-high;
contemporary accounts refer to streams of books tossed
enormously by drafts of heat onto nearby mountains . . .

in 1810, Johnes rebuilt, including a Pleasure Dome
by John Nash as North Wing—being the very one S. T. Coleridge
saw and remembered later in Somerset one porlock-personed day . . .

in 1811, Marianne, the beloved, only child, died

in 1932, Chantrey's great monument in the Church near Hafod
was destroyed by fire, the firemen
foolishly hosing down the hot marble—

Johnes' head now lies to the right, at the base,
streaks of black and ochre quite covering it . . .

in 1958, the Forestry Commission dynamited Hafod as
"a menace to the Public Safety"

in 1966, there is a caravan site where Hafod, where
Eden stood . . .

from Kubla Khan
to Caravan

a stately,
measured

doom,

decreed . . .

hoo hoo
hee hee
say the locals!

The Gaze

> *"Dwelling with things of a different nature*
> *is no remedy for exile. Notwithstanding the*
> *plants and beasts in a garden, a man can be*
> *lonely there."*
> —THOMAS AQUINAS

St. George's Day,
and Shakespeare's birthday
on another Cambrian river:

April 23, 1695,
In the 73rd Year of His Age,

HENRY VAUGHAN, M.D.

THE SWAN OF USK; SWEET PSALMIST
OF ISRAEL; KNOWN ALSO
AS THE SILURIST,

Rest in Peace,
said a late Victorian tablet . . .

Vaughan's slab in the churchyard at Llansantffraed
is of the Old Red Sandstone,
but the A-40, Llansantffraed to Brecon,
runs along on Silurian pebbles
under the Gilded Clouds
where he his eys did pour
Upon a flowr,

        rhymed with *bowres* and *houres*
        for any number of Neo-Platonic *years,*

for flowres gather'd in this world
die here

and white Celestiall thoughts
of yellow Celandines are naught . . .

GLORY!
HAVE MERCY!
suggests
the inscription . . .

FROM: BLUES & ROOTS/RUE & BLUETS

A book still in the works. It is a Garland For the Appalachians: 100 poems and 100 photographs by Nicholas Dean. We have been working on it five years and intend to get it done right. The specimens here come from two kinds of poem: (1) common words in uncommon orders— conversations quoted exactly but cast into line to reveal their native invention; (2) signs, observed, and cast into typography to let them work on those not lucky enough to have seen them in the first place. The book is dedicated to William Bartram, for Franklinia Alatamaha; André Michaux, for Shortia Galicifolia; and Charles Ives, for Everything.

Bea Hensley Hammers an Iron Chinquapin Leaf
On His Anvil Near Spruce Pine
& Cogitates on the Nature of Two Beauty Spots

in the Linville Gorge I
know this place

now it's a rock wall
you look up
it's covered in punktatum all
the way to Heaven

that's a
sight!
•
up on Smoky
you ease up at daybust
and see the first
light in the tops of the tulip trees

now boys that just naturally
grinds and polishes
the soul

makes it
normal
again

I mean it's really
pretty!

The Hermit Cackleberry Brown, On Human Vanity:

caint call your name
but your face is easy

come sit

now some folks figure theyre
bettern
cowflop they
aint

not a bit

just good to hold the world together
like hooved up ground

thats what

Old Man Sam Ward's History of the Gee-Haw Whimmy-Diddle

some folks say
the injuns made 'em
like lie detectors
called'em
hoo-doo sticks

feller
in Salisbury, North Caylini
mide the first
whimmy-diddle I seen

I whittle seven
kind: thisuns king
size, thisuns jumbo, thisuns
extry large

here's a single, here's one
double, here's a triple and why right here
here's a forked 'un

been whittlin' whimmy-diddles come
ten year, I reckon you'd
care to see my other toys,
boys, I got some fine
flipper-dingers, fly-
killers and bull-roarers, I can

kill a big fly at 60 feet

watch here

Lee Ogle Ties a Broom & Ponders Cures for Arthuritis

lands them fingers really
dreadfulled me I
couldnt tie
nary broom one

had to soak em in water
hot as birds blood

then I heared this ol man from Kentucky say
take a jug of apple juice just juice not cider
pour the epsum salts to it and
take as much as you kin

bein fleshy I kin take
right smart but
boys you know it moves a mans bowels
somethin terrible

well boys it just
naturally killed that arthuritis
lost me some weight too
and I
still tie thesehere brooms

pretty good

Daddy Bostain, the Moses of the Wing Community Moonshiners,
Laments from His Deathbed the Spiritual Estate
Of One of His Soul-Saving Neighbors:

> God bless her pore
> little ol
> dried up
> soul!
>
> jest make
> good kindlin wood
> fer Hell . . .

The September Satisfaction of Uncle Iv Owens:

> I got
> a rat-proof
> crib!

The Custodian of a Field of Whisky Bushes
By the Nolichucky River Speaks:

took me a pecka real ripe tomaters up
into the Grassy Gap
one night

and two quarts of good stockade
and just laid there

sippin and tastin and lookin agin the moon
at them sort of fish eyes in the jar
you get when its right

boys Im talkin bout somethin
good

Snuffy Smith's Colossal Maw From War-Woman Dell

more mouth on
that woman

than ass
on a goose

Laments From the Pigeon Roost News

once we all grew shellot
potato onions everybody
around here have run out of
seed E.E. Seaton
of Jonesboro
Tennessee done heard
about this

•

the Fourth a July
Holiday
passed off in this part
very quiet

•

that snake were such
peculiar looking
to me I'm afraid I
couldn't give it justice
trying to describing it but it
didn't act mean like
it tryed to be
pretty like
it did

The Nostrums of the Black Mountain Publican

best thing
for roomatiz,
Homer, is

a great big ol messa
Woolly-Booger

if God
made anything better
he kep it
for Hissef

but, boys, lemme
tell you:

DON'T EAT NO
HAIRPIE
ON FRIDAY!

Uncle Iv Surveys His Domain From His Rocker of a Sunday
Afternoon As Aunt Dory Starts to Chop Kindling

> Mister Williams
> lets youn me move
> tother side the house
>
> the woman
> choppin woods
> mite nigh the awkerdist thing
> I seen

Mrs. Sadie Grindstaff, Weaver & Factotum,
Explains the Work-Principle to the Modern World

> I figured
> anything anybody
> could do a lot of I
> could do a little
> of
>
> mebby

Three Sayings From Highlands, North Carolina

but pretty though as
roses is
you can put up with
the thorns
— *Doris Talley, Housewife & Gardener*

•

you live until you die—
if the limb don't fall
— *Butler Jenkins, Caretaker*

•

your points is blue
and your timing's
a week off
— *Sam Creswell, Auto Mechanic*

Granny Donaldson Scoffs at Skeptics & the Uninitiated
As She Works up a Cow-Blanket
(Of Homespun, Crocheting & Appliqué)
Up a Branch Near Brasstown

QUESTION: whut fer
thesehyar
animules
be,
Granny?

ANSWER: haint fer
to name! why Adam's
Off-Ox
in thishyar
Garden
haint got
no name
neither
yet

but the Lord's
liable to call
thishyar
tree
Arber
Vity

hit's got
thishyar
sarpint
in it

From Uncle Jake Carpenter's Anthology
of Death on Three-Mile Creek

Loney Ollis
age 84
dide jun 10 1871

grates dere honter
wreked bee trees for hony
cild ratell snak by 100
cild dere by thousen

i nod him well

The Ancient of Days

would that I
had known Aunt Cumi
Woody

C-u-m-i, pronounced
Q-my

she lived in the Deyton Bend Section of Mitchell
County, North Carolina many years ago

there is one of Bayard Wootten's photographs of her
standing there smiling with her store-bought
teeth, holding a coverlet

she sheared her sheep, spun
and dyed her yarn in vegetable dyes,
and wove the coverlet

in indigo, the brown from walnut roots,
red from madder, green from hickory ooze, first,
then into the indigo (the blue pot)

Cumi, from the Bible
(St. Mark 5:41)

Talitha Cumi:
'Damsel, I say unto thee, arise!'

she is gone, she
enjoyed her days

The Epitaph on Uncle Nick Grindstaff's Grave
On the Iron Mountain Above Shady Valley, Tennessee:

LIVED ALONE   SUFFERED ALONE   DIED ALONE

Paint Sign on a Rough Rock
Yonside of Boone Side of Shady Valley:

BEPREPA
REDTO
MEETGO
D

Jeff Brooks, Wagon-Master of Andrews,
En Route to Franklin Through the Nantahalas:

no
other
sound

except

the creak
of leather

Aubade

you could hear an ant
fart
it was that
quiet

What Are the Names
Of the Three Tutelary Hamadryads
Of the Hickory Grove
On Dirty John Creek in the Nantahalas?

   BUSTHAID

   BLOCKADE

   POPSKULL

A Pileated Woodpecker's Response to Four Dogwood Berries:

   (1) kuk

   (2) kuk   kuk

   (3) kuk-kuk

   (4) kukkuk

The Traditionally Accommodating Spirit of the Mountains
Shows Up in Neon in Franklin, NC, Once Nikwasi, a Cherokee
Capital:

   CAFÉ

The Yellow Peril at Moore's Grocery

   COLD
   BEER
   TOGO

John Chapman Pulls Off the Highway
Towards Kentucky and Casts a Cold Eye
On the Most Astonishing Sign in Recent American Letters:

   O'NAN'S
    AUTO
   SERVICE